Brainteasers

Brainteasers

200 Challenging Puzzles

ARCTURUS

ARCTURUS

This edition published in 2012 by Arcturus Publishing Limited
26/27 Bickels Yard, 151–153 Bermondsey Street,
London SE1 3HA

ISBN: 978-1-84858-624-6
AD002259EN

Printed in China

Contents

DOMINO PLACEMENT

A standard set of 28 dominoes has been laid out as shown. Can you draw in the edges of them all? The check-box is provided as an aid and the domino already placed will help.

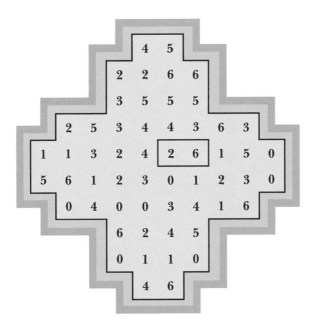

0-0	0-1	0-2	0-3	0-4	0-5	0-6	1-1	1-2	1-3	1-4	1-5	1-6	2-2

2-3	2-4	2-5	2-6	3-3	3-4	3-5	3-6	4-4	4-5	4-6	5-5	5-6	6-6
			✓										

BALANCING THE SCALES

2   Given that scales A and B balance perfectly, how many diamonds are needed to balance scale C?

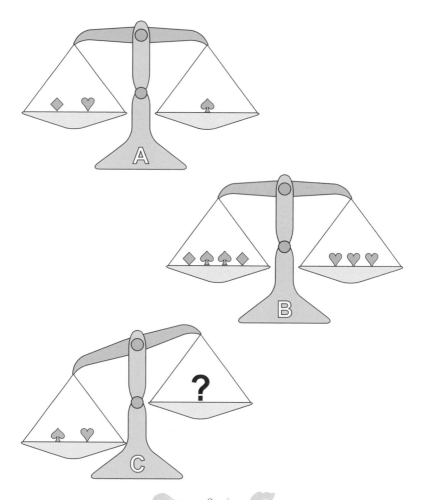

SHAPE UP

Every row and column in this grid originally contained one heart, one club, one diamond, one spade and two blank squares, although not necessarily in that order.

3

Every symbol with a black arrow refers to the first of the four symbols encountered when travelling in the direction of the arrow. Every symbol with a white arrow refers to the second of the four symbols encountered in the direction of the arrow.

Can you complete the original grid?

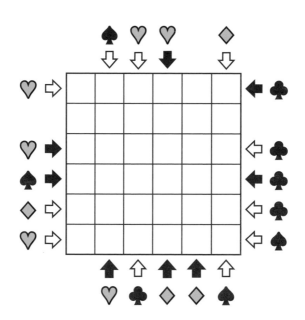

TOTAL CONCENTRATION

4

The blank squares below should be filled with whole numbers between 1 and 30 inclusive, any of which may occur more than once, or not at all.

The numbers in every horizontal row add up to the totals on the right, as do the two long diagonal lines; whilst those in every vertical column add up to the totals along the bottom.

							91
	3	14	3	22	7		106
10	6		6	21	2	13	73
5	20	16	2	4		29	88
	30			14	26	7	106
18	9	4	8		19		94
10		1	12		1	11	83
15		9	16	17		24	116
90	111	72	58	109	84	142	93

WHATEVER NEXT?

Draw in the missing hands on the final clock.

5

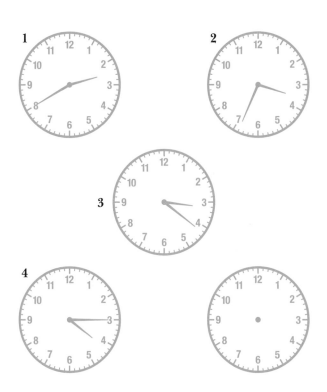

HEXAGONY

6 Can you place the hexagons into the grid, so that where any hexagon touches another along a straight line, the number in both triangles is the same? No rotation of any hexagon is allowed!

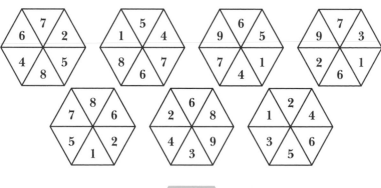

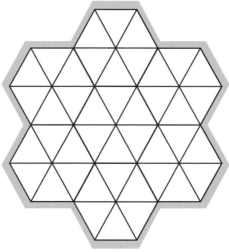

Ls in Place

Twelve L-shapes like the ones here need to be inserted in the grid and each L has one hole in it.

There are three pieces of each of the four kinds shown here and any piece may be turned or flipped over before being put in the grid. No pieces of the same kind may touch, even at a corner.

The pieces fit together so well that you cannot see any spaces between them; only the holes show.

Can you tell where the Ls are? One is already in place.

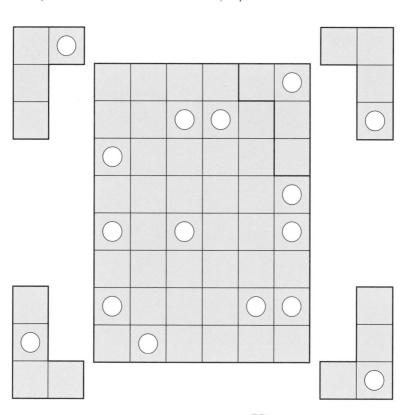

COIN COLLECTING

8

In this puzzle, an amateur coin collector has been out with his metal detector, searching for booty. He didn't have time to dig up all the coins he found, so he made a grid map, showing their locations, in the hope that if he loses the map, at least no-one else will be able to understand it…

Those squares containing numbers are empty, but where a number appears in a square, it indicates how many coins are located in the squares (up to a maximum of eight) surrounding the numbered one, touching it at any corner or side. There is only one coin in any individual square.

Place a circle into every square containing a coin.

						0			1
	4		3		2				2
	2		3	4					1
		5				4			
			3			1			
1	4				2		4	2	
			2						1
2			3		3				
	5							5	
	3			2	3				2

LATIN SQUARE

The grid should be filled with numbers from 1 to 6, so that each number appears just once in every row and column. The clues refer to the digit totals in the squares, eg A 1 2 3 = 6 means that the numbers in squares A1, A2 and A3 add up to 6.

9

1 E F 4 = 7	**7** B C 1 = 5
2 F 3 4 = 9	**8** E 1 2 3 = 6
3 D E 6 = 10	**9** A B 2 = 5
4 B 3 4 = 6	**10** E 5 6 = 11
5 C D 5 = 4	**11** D E 4 = 9
6 F 2 3 4 = 14	**12** A 3 4 5 = 13

	A	B	C	D	E	F
1						
2						
3						
4						
5						
6						

Simple as A, B, C?

10 Each of the small squares in the grid below contains either A, B or C. Every row and column has exactly two of each letter, as do the two long diagonal lines of six squares. Can you tell the letter in each square?

Across

1 The As are further left than the Bs.

2 The As are further right than the Bs.

3 The Bs are between the Cs.

4 The Bs are further left than the As.

5 The As are further right than the Cs.

6 The Cs are between the Bs.

Down

1 The Cs are between the As.

2 The As are higher than the Bs.

3 The Bs are higher than the As.

4 The Bs are higher than the Cs.

5 The Bs are lower than the Cs.

6 The Cs are between the Bs.

	1	2	3	4	5	6
1						
2						
3						
4						
5						
6						

ZIGZAG

The object of this puzzle is to trace a single path from the top left corner to the bottom right corner of the grid, travelling through all of the cells in either a horizontal, vertical or diagonal direction.

Every cell must be entered once only and your path should take you through the numbers in the sequence 1-2-3-4-5-6-1-2-3-4-5-6, etc.

Can you find the way?

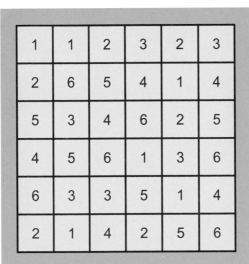

1	1	2	3	2	3
2	6	5	4	1	4
5	3	4	6	2	5
4	5	6	1	3	6
6	3	3	5	1	4
2	1	4	2	5	6

12

Can you place the vessels into the diagram? Some parts of vessels or sea squares have already been filled in. A number to the right or below a row or column refers to the number of occupied squares in that row or column.

Any vessel may be positioned horizontally or vertically, but no part of a vessel touches part of any other vessel, either horizontally, vertically or diagonally.

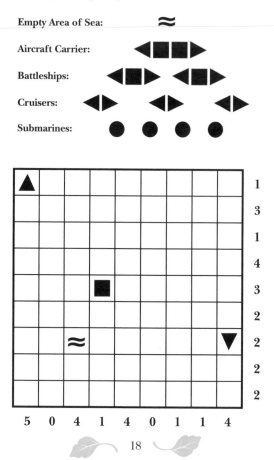

THE BOTTOM LINE

Can you fill each square in the bottom line with the correct digit?

Every square in the solution contains only one digit from the lines above, although two or more squares in the solution may contain the same digit.

13

At the end of every row is a score, which shows:

a the number of digits placed in the correct finishing position on the bottom line, as indicated by a tick; and

b the number of digits which appear on the bottom line, but in a different position, as indicated by a cross.

SCORE

3	5	6	1	✗ ✗
8	7	1	3	✗ ✗
2	4	7	8	✗ ✗
4	3	5	7	✗ ✗
7	2	1	4	✗ ✗
				✓ ✓ ✓ ✓

SLITHERLINK

14 Draw a single continuous loop, by connecting the dots. No line may cross the path of another.

The figure inside each set of any four surrounding dots indicates the total number of surrounding lines.

```
2  2  2        3  2  1  2  2
   2  2        1  0  1
2  1     1        1     3  2
2  2        2  0  2  1  1  1
2  1
1        2  3        3
2        3        0           1
      0     1  2  1  1
3        2  1  2  1           1
2  1     1     1  1     2
2     2     1  2  3  1  1  3
2  2  3  2  3     1        2
```

COMBIKU

Each horizontal row and vertical column should contain different shapes and different numbers.

Every square will contain one number and one shape and no combination may be repeated anywhere else in the puzzle.

15

◇ ○ ☆ ⬡ □

1   2   3   4   5

4	2	□	⬡	
3				
		⬡1		5
☆			3	
○				3

WHATEVER NEXT?

16 In the diagram below, which letter should replace the question mark?

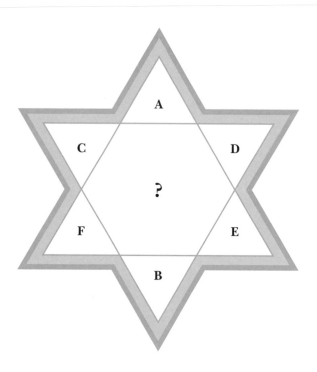

ADDING UP

In the square below, change the positions of six numbers, one per horizontal row, vertical column and long diagonal line of six smaller squares, in such a way that the numbers in each row, column and long diagonal line total exactly 98. Any number may appear more than once in a row, column or line.

17

18	4	17	12	14	10
19	16	20	14	18	24
15	37	16	12	5	21
15	23	18	22	9	13
9	18	23	22	12	7
29	8	17	18	17	16

18 Given that the letters are valued 1-26 according to their respective places in the alphabet, can you crack the mystery code to reveal the missing letter?

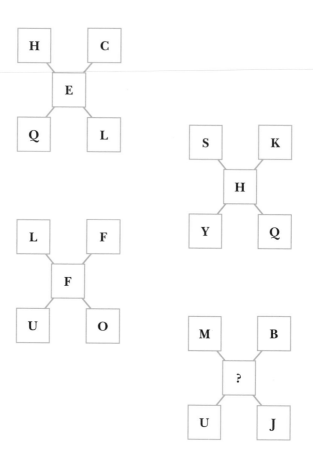

DOMINOLOGICAL

A set of dominoes is to be placed in four rows as shown below. The numbers indicate which values are shown on all the dominoes in each column and the relevant half of the domino in every row. Find out where each domino is placed by carefully comparing rows and columns to determine the possible positions of certain dominoes: for instance, if any column contains only one 6, then the domino 6/6 isn't in that column.

A set of dominoes consists of:

0/0, 0/1, 0/2, 0/3, 0/4, 0/5, 0/6, 1/1, 1/2, 1/3, 1/4, 1/5, 1/6, 2/2, 2/3, 2/4, 2/5, 2/6, 3/3, 3/4, 3/5, 3/6, 4/4, 4/5, 4/6, 5/5, 5/6, 6/6.

	0, 1, 1, 2, 4, 4, 5, 6.	1, 1, 1, 1, 2, 3, 5, 6.	0, 0, 1, 3, 3, 6, 6, 6.	0, 1, 3, 3, 4, 4, 4, 6.	0, 0, 2, 2, 2, 3, 4, 5.	0, 2, 2, 2, 4, 4, 5, 5.	0, 3, 3, 5, 5, 5, 6, 6.
0, 0, 1, 4, 4, 6, 6.							
0, 2, 2, 2, 5, 5, 6.							
1, 2, 3, 4, 4, 5, 5.							3
1, 2, 3, 3, 3, 4, 4.							3
0, 1, 3, 3, 3, 6, 6.							
0, 0, 0, 1, 2, 2, 6.							
0, 1, 1, 4, 5, 5, 6.							
1, 2, 3, 4, 5, 5, 6.							

TILE TWISTER

20 Place the eight tiles into the puzzle grid so that all adjacent numbers on each tile match up. Tiles may be rotated through 360 degrees, but none may be flipped over.

3	1
1	1

4	2
3	1

2	3
2	3

1	2
1	3

1	3
3	1

3	3
1	4

4	3
1	1

2	1
3	2

1	2				
3	4				

PIECEWORK

Place all twelve of the pieces into the grid. Any may be rotated or flipped over, but none may touch another, not even diagonally. The numbers outside the grid refer to the number of consecutive black squares; and each block is separated from the others by at least one white square. For instance, '3 2' could refer to a row with none, one or more white squares, then three black squares, then at least one white square, then two more black squares, followed by any number of white squares.

					1	1								3		
					1	3	1		2	2				1		
			2	1	2	1	2	1	3				1	1
			2	2	1	1	1	2	1	1	1	2	3
			1	2	1	1	1	1	1	1	1	1	3

| 4 3 |
| 1 1 |
| 2 1 |
| 1 2 |
| 3 1 2 |
| 1 1 |
| 1 1 2 |
| 3 1 |
| 1 3 2 |
| 1 2 |
| 3 1 |
| 1 1 |
| 4 |
| 2 |
| 3 5 |

Number Fill

22

With the starter already given, can you fit all of the remaining listed numbers into this grid? Take care, this puzzle may not be as easy as it looks!

19	116	756	3848	8231	114404
23	194	784	4236	8629	211255
34	254	893	4681✓	9340	241463
37	307	895	4682	9377	319244
43	354	925	5767	9424	456978
48	415	930	6560	9729	483681
56	563	1397	6580	18496	547633
64	571	2705	7026	32864	569956
74	660	2727	7052	55396	603891
89	702	3828	7647	92174	638179

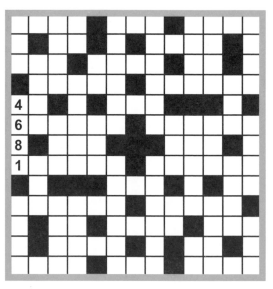

PYRAMID PLUS

Every brick in this pyramid contains a number which is the sum of the two numbers below it, so that F=A+B, etc. Just work out the missing numbers!

23

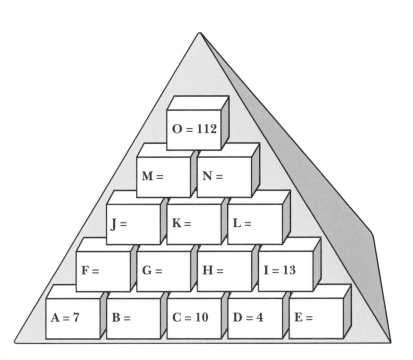

O = 112

M =   N =

J =   K =   L =

F =   G =   H =   I = 13

A = 7   B =   C = 10   D = 4   E =

TREASURE HUNT

24

The chart gives directions to a hidden treasure behind the centre black square in the grid. Move the indicated number of spaces north, south, east and west (eg 4N means move four squares north) stopping at every square once only to arrive there. At which square should you start?

N

1E	1E	2S	1E	2S
1S	1W	1E	2S	2W
2N	2E	■	2N	1N
2E	2N	1W	1E	1S
1N	1W	1E	2W	2W

W

E

S

FUTOSHIKI

Fill the grid so that every horizontal row and vertical column contains the numbers 1-5. The 'greater than' or 'less than' signs indicate where a number is larger or smaller than that in the neighbouring square.

 25

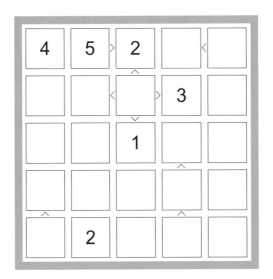

SPIDOKU

26 Each of the eight segments of the spider's web should be filled with a different number from 1 to 8, in such a way that every ring also contains a different number from 1 to 8. The segments run from the outside of the spider's web to the centre, and the rings run all the way around. Some numbers are already in place. Can you fill in the rest?

LETTER LOCATOR

Every oval shape in this diagram contains a different letter of the alphabet from A to K inclusive. Use the clues to determine their locations. Reference in the clues to 'due' means in any location along the same horizontal or vertical line.

1 The A is due north of the B, which is due west of the F.

2 The E is due east of the D, and due south of the I.

3 The F is further south than the G, which is due west of the J.

4 The G is due north of the K, which is due west of the F.

5 The J is due north of the H, which is next to and due north of the C.

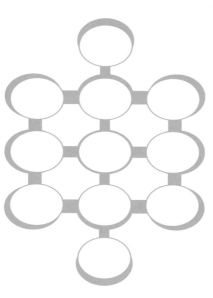

SUM CIRCLE

28

Fill the three empty circles with the symbols +, – and x in some order, to make a sum which totals the number in the centre. Each symbol must be used once and calculations are made in the direction of travel (clockwise).

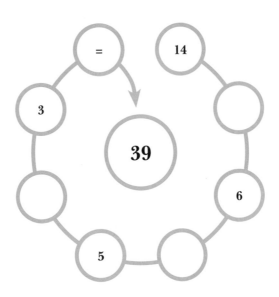

ONE TO NINE

Using the numbers below, complete these six equations (three reading across and three reading downwards). Every number is used once.

1   3   4
5   6   8   9

7	+		÷		=	4
+	■	−	■	−		
	−		x	2	=	14
−	■	x	■	+		
	x		+		=	33
=		=		=		
11		24		10		

WORK IT OUT

30

In the grid below, which number should replace the question mark?

24	32	47	11	41	6	19
36	7	26	34	15	45	10
18	1	12	30	5	25	33
21	37	27	20	42	31	17
3	23	43	9	?	13	38
40	39	29	2	22	49	4
14	8	48	44	16	46	28

Symbol Sums

Each symbol stands for a different number. In order to reach the correct total at the end of each row and column, what is the value of the circle, cross, pentagon, square and star?

31

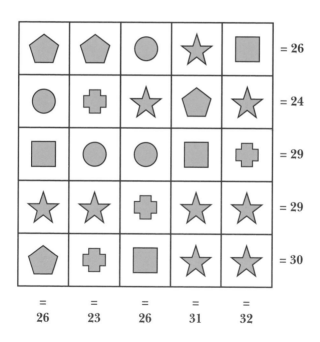

Logi-6

32 Every row and column of this grid should contain one each of the numbers 1, 2, 3, 4, 5 and 6. Each of the six shapes (marked by thicker lines) should also contain one each of the numbers 1, 2, 3, 4, 5 and 6. Can you complete the grid?

	1				
		4		5	
		5	1	6	4
		6			
			4		1
				2	

A standard set of 28 dominoes has been laid out as shown. Can you draw in the edges of them all? The check-box is provided as an aid and the domino already placed will help.

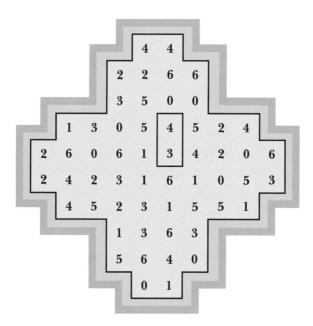

0-0	0-1	0-2	0-3	0-4	0-5	0-6	1-1	1-2	1-3	1-4	1-5	1-6	2-2

2-3	2-4	2-5	2-6	3-3	3-4	3-5	3-6	4-4	4-5	4-6	5-5	5-6	6-6
					✔								

JIGSAW

34 Which four pieces can be fitted together to form an exact copy of this shape?

A

B

C

D

E

F

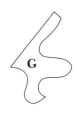

G

H

I

J

SHAPE UP

Every row and column in this grid originally contained one heart, one club, one diamond, one spade and two blank squares, although not necessarily in that order.

Every symbol with a black arrow refers to the first of the four symbols encountered when travelling in the direction of the arrow. Every symbol with a white arrow refers to the second of the four symbols encountered in the direction of the arrow.

Can you complete the original grid?

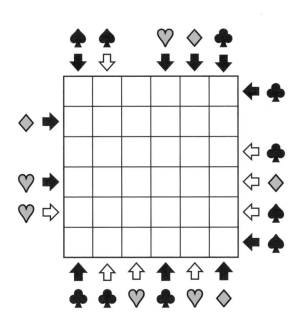

36

The blank squares below should be filled with whole numbers between 1 and 30 inclusive, any of which may occur more than once, or not at all.

The numbers in every horizontal row add up to the totals on the right, as do the two long diagonal lines; whilst those in every vertical column add up to the totals along the bottom.

							117
	23	6	30	7	22		130
1		5	16	4	10		81
15	14	19		29		2	130
9		24		26	3	28	139
20	8		26		21	27	107
	13	3	12	6	2	11	72
24	5		18	27		19	128
119	115	89	152	100	86	126	109

COMPARISONS

Look at figures A and B, comparing the two, then try to discover which of the three alternatives (D, E or F) most closely follows the pattern in relation to C.

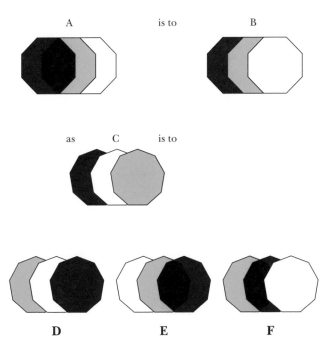

A   is to   B

as   C   is to

D   **E**   **F**

HEXAGONY

38 Can you place the hexagons into the grid, so that where any hexagon touches another along a straight line, the number in both triangles is the same? No rotation of any hexagon is allowed!

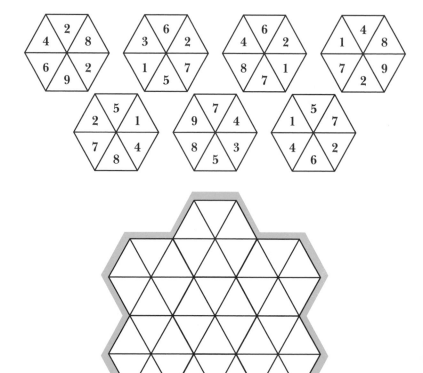

Ls in Place

Twelve L-shapes like the ones here need to be inserted in the grid and each L has one hole in it.

There are three pieces of each of the four kinds shown here and any piece may be turned or flipped over before being put in the grid. No pieces of the same kind may touch, even at a corner.

The pieces fit together so well that you cannot see any spaces between them; only the holes show.

Can you tell where the Ls are?

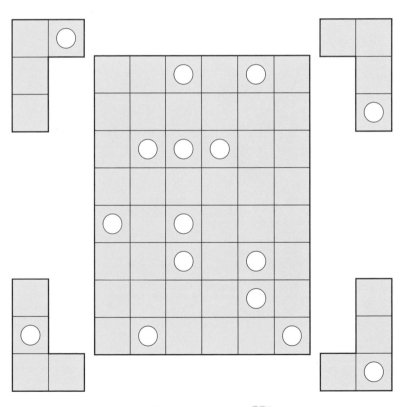

COIN COLLECTING

40

In this puzzle, an amateur coin collector has been out with his metal detector, searching for booty. He didn't have time to dig up all the coins he found, so he made a grid map, showing their locations, in the hope that if he loses the map, at least no-one else will be able to understand it…

Those squares containing numbers are empty, but where a number appears in a square, it indicates how many coins are located in the squares (up to a maximum of eight) surrounding the numbered one, touching it at any corner or side. There is only one coin in any individual square.

Place a circle into every square containing a coin.

	1		1	0					
	2					2	3		3
	3		2	1					2
			3	4		3	1	3	
3		6					0	2	
2						2	1		
		4	4				2	3	
		3					2		
2	3			1	0		2	3	3
0									

LATIN SQUARE

The grid should be filled with numbers from 1 to 6, so that each number appears just once in every row and column. The clues refer to the digit totals in the squares, eg A 1 2 3 = 6 means that the numbers in squares A1, A2 and A3 add up to 6.

1 E 3 4 5 = 15
2 B 2 3 4 = 6
3 F 3 4 5 = 9
4 D E 2 = 6
5 C D 1 = 10
6 B C 3 = 3

7 D 2 3 4 = 12
8 E F 4 = 7
9 A 1 2 = 3
10 B C 2 = 9
11 B C D 6 = 8
12 E F 5 = 8

	A	B	C	D	E	F
1						
2						
3						
4						
5						
6						

SIMPLE AS **A, B, C?**

42 Each of the small squares in the grid below contains either A, B or C. Every row and column has exactly two of each letter, as do the two long diagonal lines of six squares. Can you tell the letter in each square?

Across

1 The Bs are further left than the Cs.

2 The As are further left than the Bs.

3 The Cs are between the As.

6 The Bs are between the Cs.

Down

1 The Bs are higher than the As.

2 The As are higher than the Cs.

4 The Cs are between the Bs.

5 The As are between the Bs.

6 The Cs are between the As.

	1	2	3	4	5	6
1						
2						
3						
4						
5						
6						

ZIGZAG

The object of this puzzle is to trace a single path from the top left corner to the bottom right corner of the grid, travelling through all of the cells in either a horizontal, vertical or diagonal direction.

Every cell must be entered once only and your path should take you through the numbers in the sequence 1-2-3-4-5-6-1-2-3-4-5-6, etc.

Can you find the way?

1	4	5	1	3	4
2	3	1	6	2	5
4	6	2	3	4	6
5	3	5	5	3	1
2	6	6	4	2	5
1	1	2	3	4	6

BATTLESHIPS

44

Can you place the vessels into the diagram? Some parts of vessels or sea squares have already been filled in. A number to the right or below a row or column refers to the number of occupied squares in that row or column.

Any vessel may be positioned horizontally or vertically, but no part of a vessel touches part of any other vessel, either horizontally, vertically or diagonally.

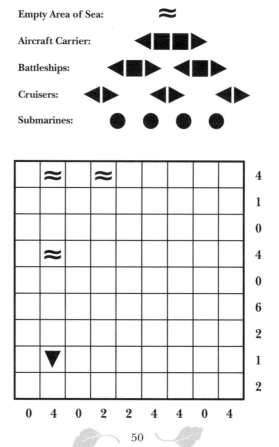

THE BOTTOM LINE

Can you fill each square in the bottom line with the correct digit?

Every square in the solution contains only one digit from the lines above, although two or more squares in the solution may contain the same digit.

45

At the end of every row is a score, which shows:

  a the number of digits placed in the correct finishing position on the bottom line, as indicated by a tick; and

  b the number of digits which appear on the bottom line, but in a different position, as indicated by a cross.

SCORE

5	9	9	7	✗
2	9	4	6	✓
8	6	3	3	✗ ✗
3	5	7	8	✗ ✗
7	8	5	9	✗ ✗
				✓ ✓ ✓ ✓

SLITHERLINK

46

Draw a single continuous loop, by connecting the dots. No line may cross the path of another.

The figure inside each set of any four surrounding dots indicates the total number of surrounding lines.

```
    3  2  2  2     2  1  2
 2  1  0  1        1     3  1
              1  1              2
       2      1  1  1  2        2
 2  1  2  1  3  2     1  2
 1     2  0  2        2  1  1
 2           1  2
       1                 2
    2        2  2  0  2     3
 2  2  2  3  1     2  1
 2  0  1  1        2     1  1
 2  2     2  2  2     2
```

COMBIKU

Each horizontal row and vertical column should contain different shapes and different numbers.

Every square will contain one number and one shape and no combination may be repeated anywhere else in the puzzle.

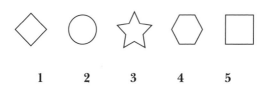

1   2   3   4   5

□		1	⬡5	◇
5			◇	
	□	5		⬡
⬡	◇	○	☆4	
		⬡	2	○

WHATEVER NEXT?

48 In the diagram below, which number should replace the question mark?

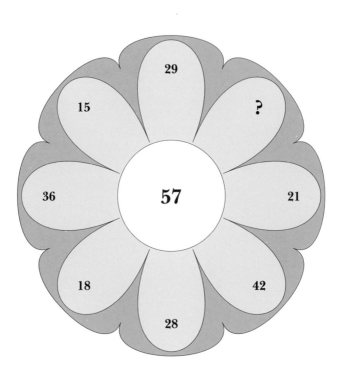

ADDING UP

In the square below, change the positions of six numbers, one per
horizontal row, vertical column and long diagonal line of six smaller
squares, in such a way that the numbers in each row, column and
long diagonal line total exactly 111. Any number may appear more
than once in a row, column or line.

49

32	7	4	1	24	21
29	31	2	3	22	23
12	9	17	26	28	25
10	11	18	19	36	27
13	16	30	33	5	8
14	15	34	35	6	20

50 Given that the letters are valued 1-26 according to their respective places in the alphabet, can you crack the mystery code to reveal the missing letter?

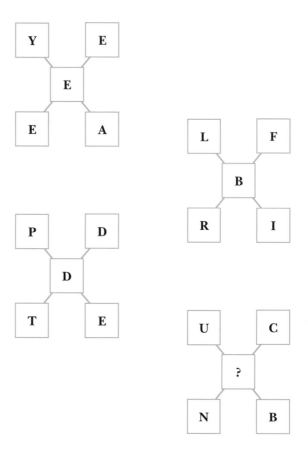

WHATEVER NEXT?

Which of the four lettered alternatives (A, B, C or D) fits most
logically into the empty square?

51

7	8	2
9	6	4
11	3	7

5	8	4
10	6	3
1	5	15

12	1	4
3	7	9
6	13	2

?

2	3	13
4	9	5
10	6	7

A

2	7	8
5	6	9
4	5	13

B

9	3	5
1	8	10
9	5	7

C

10	2	6
4	8	7
11	8	3

D

TILE TWISTER

52 Place the eight tiles into the puzzle grid so that all adjacent numbers on each tile match up. Tiles may be rotated through 360 degrees, but none may be flipped over.

4	2
4	3

2	3
4	1

1	3
4	1

1	3
3	2

4	1
4	2

2	4
3	3

2	4
3	2

4	3
4	4

		4	3		
		1	2		

PIECEWORK

Place all twelve of the pieces into the grid. Any may be rotated or flipped over, but none may touch another, not even diagonally. The numbers outside the grid refer to the number of consecutive black squares; and each block is separated from the others by at least one white square. For instance, '3 2' could refer to a row with none, one or more white squares, then three black squares, then at least one white square, then two more black squares, followed by any number of white squares.

53

					2		1		2			
				1	1		2		2		3	1	
			2	2	3	2	5	2	1	2	1	4	1
			1	3	1	1	3	1	1	3	1	1	4
1	1	1											
3	3	1											
1	1	3											
		3											
	2	2											
		2											
1	1	1	1										
	1	1	2										
	2	1	1										
	1	1	1										
		1	2										
	1	1	2										
3	1	2	1										
	1	1	1										
		3	1										

59

NUMBER FILL

54

With the starters already given, can you fit all of the remaining listed numbers into this grid? Take care, this puzzle may not be as easy as it looks!

26	210	479	851	10621	75801
36	275	505	860	12417	94721
47	284	525	862	13342	181213
70	308	587	950	16976	185620
71	380	611	3285	17581	291153
74	405	621	3366 ✓	31892	297135
86	406	671	4111	42855	635874
90	443	755	5746	50000	712310
132	446	788	6114	63413	716414
191	458	800	7114	65163	836871

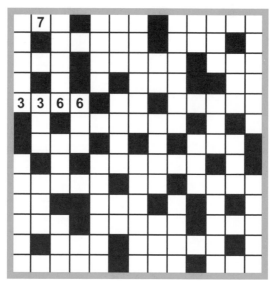

PYRAMID PLUS

Every brick in this pyramid contains a number which is the sum
of the two numbers below it, so that F=A+B, etc. Just work out the
missing numbers!

55

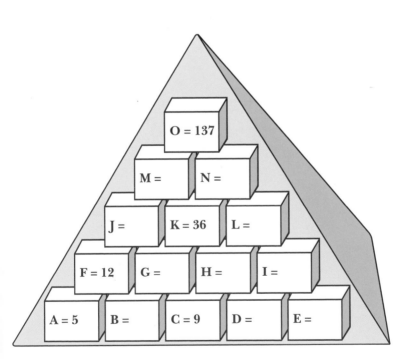

TREASURE HUNT

56

The chart gives directions to a hidden treasure behind the centre black square in the grid. Move the indicated number of spaces north, south, east and west (eg 4N means move four squares north) stopping at every square once only to arrive there. At which square should you start?

N

1E	1S	1E	1S	2W
1N	1E	2E	1S	2S
1N	1E	■	1S	2N
2E	1N	1W	1S	1S
1N	1E	2W	2W	2N

W

E

S

FUTOSHIKI

Fill the grid so that every horizontal row and vertical column contains the numbers 1-5. The 'greater than' or 'less than' signs indicate where a number is larger or smaller than that in the neighbouring square.

57

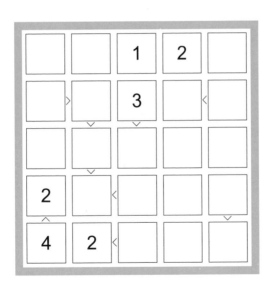

58 Each of the eight segments of the spider's web should be filled with a different number from 1 to 8, in such a way that every ring also contains a different number from 1 to 8. The segments run from the outside of the spider's web to the centre, and the rings run all the way around. Some numbers are already in place. Can you fill in the rest?

LETTER LOCATOR

Every oval shape in this diagram contains a different letter of the alphabet from A to K inclusive. Use the clues to determine their locations. Reference in the clues to 'due' means in any location along the same horizontal or vertical line.

1 The A is due south of the F, which is due south of the I, which is due east of the G.

2 The B is next to and due north of the E, which is due east of the C.

3 The D is due east of the K, and due north of the J.

4 The H is due north of the D, which is further south than the E.

5 The J is further west than the A.

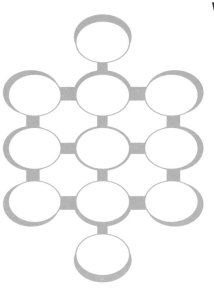

SUM CIRCLE

60 Fill the three empty circles with the symbols +, – and x in some order, to make a sum which totals the number in the centre. Each symbol must be used once and calculations are made in the direction of travel (clockwise).

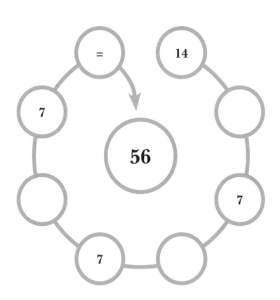

ONE TO NINE

Using the numbers below, complete these six equations (three reading across and three reading downwards). Every number is used once.

61

		1		2		4
5		7		8		9

	x	3	−		=	4
x	■	−	■	+		
6	+		x		=	49
÷	■	x	■	÷		
	+		x		=	55
=		=		=		
12		18		3		

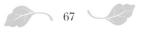

WORK IT OUT

62 In the grid below, which number should replace the question mark?

29	71	11	23	66	55	44
34	76	16	28	71	60	49
40	82	22	34	77	66	55
47	89	29	41	84	73	62
41	83	23	35	78	67	56
36	78	18	30	73	62	51
42	84	24	36	79	?	57

Symbol Sums

Each symbol stands for a different number. In order to reach the correct total at the end of each row and column, what is the value of the circle, cross, pentagon, square and star?

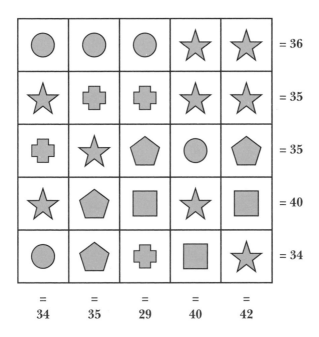

= 36
= 35
= 35
= 40
= 34

=
34
=
35
=
29
=
40
=
42

Logi-6

64 Every row and column of this grid should contain one each of the numbers 1, 2, 3, 4, 5 and 6. Each of the six shapes (marked by thicker lines) should also contain one each of the numbers 1, 2, 3, 4, 5 and 6. Can you complete the grid?

5	6		2	3	
					4
3				1	
	5				
				4	2

DOMINO PLACEMENT

A standard set of 28 dominoes has been laid out as shown. Can you draw in the edges of them all? The check-box is provided as an aid and the domino already placed will help.

0-0	0-1	0-2	0-3	0-4	0-5	0-6	1-1	1-2	1-3	1-4	1-5	1-6	2-2
											✔		

2-3	2-4	2-5	2-6	3-3	3-4	3-5	3-6	4-4	4-5	4-6	5-5	5-6	6-6

BALANCING THE SCALES

66 Given that scales A and B balance perfectly, how many spades are needed to balance scale C?

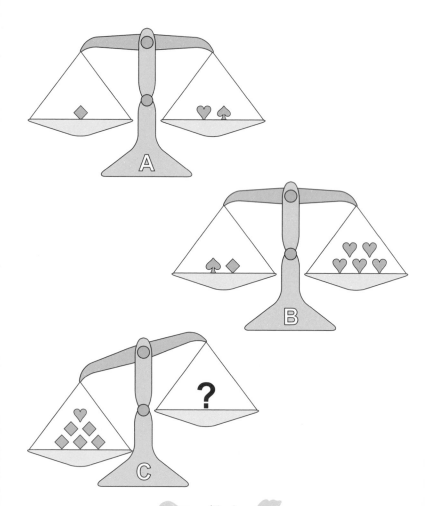

SHAPE UP

Every row and column in this grid originally contained one heart, one club, one diamond, one spade and two blank squares, although not necessarily in that order.

Every symbol with a black arrow refers to the first of the four symbols encountered when travelling in the direction of the arrow. Every symbol with a white arrow refers to the second of the four symbols encountered in the direction of the arrow.

Can you complete the original grid?

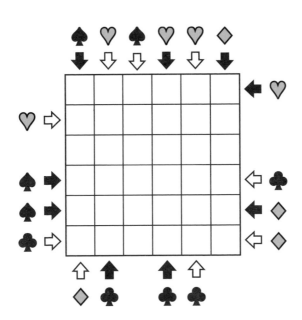

TOTAL CONCENTRATION

68

The blank squares below should be filled with whole numbers between 1 and 30 inclusive, any of which may occur more than once, or not at all.

The numbers in every horizontal row add up to the totals on the right, as do the two long diagonal lines; whilst those in every vertical column add up to the totals along the bottom.

							101
28	14		27	27	16	25	166
30		22		24	11	26	155
15	3	1		17	26		115
2		16	23	10	12	18	102
17	2	5	20	21		9	98
	1		6	4		22	74
19	6	3	20		8		109
115	**76**	**94**	**137**	**126**	**116**	**155**	**151**

WHATEVER NEXT?

Draw in the missing hands on the final clock.

69

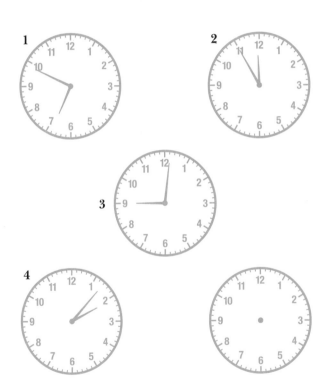

75

HEXAGONY

70 Can you place the hexagons into the grid, so that where any hexagon touches another along a straight line, the number in both triangles is the same? No rotation of any hexagon is allowed!

Ls in Place

Twelve L-shapes like the ones here need to be inserted in the grid and each L has one hole in it.

There are three pieces of each of the four kinds shown here and any piece may be turned or flipped over before being put in the grid. No pieces of the same kind may touch, even at a corner.

The pieces fit together so well that you cannot see any spaces between them; only the holes show.

Can you tell where the Ls are?

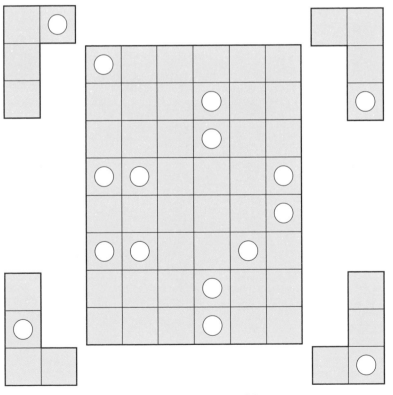

COIN COLLECTING

72

In this puzzle, an amateur coin collector has been out with his metal detector, searching for booty. He didn't have time to dig up all the coins he found, so he made a grid map, showing their locations, in the hope that if he loses the map, at least no-one else will be able to understand it…

Those squares containing numbers are empty, but where a number appears in a square, it indicates how many coins are located in the squares (up to a maximum of eight) surrounding the numbered one, touching it at any corner or side. There is only one coin in any individual square.

Place a circle into every square containing a coin.

2	2								
			3	3			4		3
	2				3			3	2
1		2	2		2			2	
	1								
2		3						4	2
		5			6				
				3			5	5	
	3			3	2	3			1
	0		1				1		

LATIN SQUARE

The grid should be filled with numbers from 1 to 6, so that each number appears just once in every row and column. The clues refer to the digit totals in the squares, eg A 1 2 3 = 6 means that the numbers in squares A1, A2 and A3 add up to 6.

73

1 A 2 3 = 8

2 D E 6 = 8

3 C 4 5 6 = 11

4 B C 5 = 3

5 F 2 3 = 8

6 E 1 2 3 = 8

7 B C D 3 = 7

8 F 4 5 = 8

9 A 4 5 6 = 10

10 C 1 2 = 8

11 D E F 5 = 14

12 A B C 2 = 11

	A	B	C	D	E	F
1						
2						
3						
4						
5						
6						

SIMPLE AS **A, B, C?**

74

Each of the small squares in the grid below contains either A, B or C. Every row and column has exactly two of each letter, as do the two long diagonal lines of six squares. Can you tell the letter in each square?

Across

1 The As are between the Cs.
2 The Cs are further left than the As.
3 Each A is directly next to and right of a C.
4 Each B is directly next to and left of a C.
5 The Cs are further left than the As.

Down

1 The Cs are higher than the Bs.
3 Any three consecutive squares contain three different letters.
4 The As are higher than the Bs.
6 The As are between the Bs.

	1	2	3	4	5	6
1						
2						
3						
4						
5						
6						

Zigzag

The object of this puzzle is to trace a single path from the top left corner to the bottom right corner of the grid, travelling through all of the cells in either a horizontal, vertical or diagonal direction.

75

Every cell must be entered once only and your path should take you through the numbers in the sequence 1-2-3-4-5-6-1-2-3-4-5-6, etc.

Can you find the way?

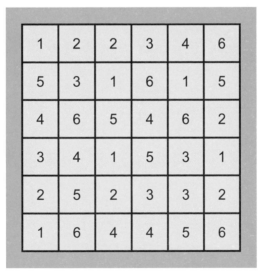

1	2	2	3	4	6
5	3	1	6	1	5
4	6	5	4	6	2
3	4	1	5	3	1
2	5	2	3	3	2
1	6	4	4	5	6

BATTLESHIPS

Can you place the vessels into the diagram? Some parts of vessels or sea squares have already been filled in. A number to the right or below a row or column refers to the number of occupied squares in that row or column.

Any vessel may be positioned horizontally or vertically, but no part of a vessel touches part of any other vessel, either horizontally, vertically or diagonally.

Empty Area of Sea:

Aircraft Carrier:

Battleships:

Cruisers:

Submarines:

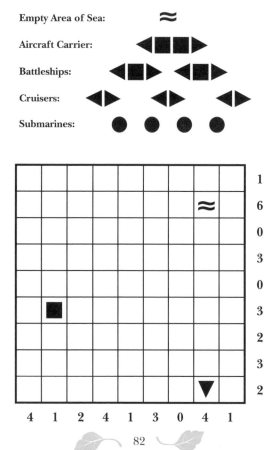

THE BOTTOM LINE

Can you fill each square in the bottom line with the correct digit?

77

Every square in the solution contains only one digit from the lines above, although two or more squares in the solution may contain the same digit.

At the end of every row is a score, which shows:

a the number of digits placed in the correct finishing position on the bottom line, as indicated by a tick; and

b the number of digits which appear on the bottom line, but in a different position, as indicated by a cross.

SCORE

1	6	9	7	✗
7	1	4	5	✗
3	2	6	9	✗ ✗
2	3	3	5	✗ ✗
5	9	2	2	✗ ✗
				✓✓✓✓

SLITHERLINK

78

Draw a single continuous loop, by connecting the dots. No line may cross the path of another.

The figure inside each set of any four surrounding dots indicates the total number of surrounding lines.

```
  2  3     2  2           3
     1  3  2     3  2     1
           1     1           2
  2  1  3  1     1  0  2     2
  2  1        2  3           2
  2        2           1  0  2
     0        2  1     3     2
  1     2  0                 2
     1        3  1  2  0  1
  3           2  1  2  2  2  3
  2     2  0     1     2  2  1
  2  2           1  2     2
```

COMBIKU

Each horizontal row and vertical column should contain different shapes and different numbers.

79

Every square will contain one number and one shape and no combination may be repeated anywhere else in the puzzle.

| 1 | 2 | 3 | 4 | 5 |

80 In the diagram below, which letter should replace the question mark?

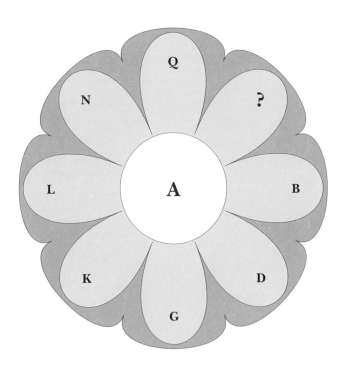

ADDING UP

In the square below, change the positions of six numbers, one per horizontal row, vertical column and long diagonal line of six smaller squares, in such a way that the numbers in each row, column and long diagonal line total exactly 122. Any number may appear more than once in a row, column or line.

81

20	32	19	26	40	8
20	20	20	19	22	8
23	25	20	16	19	30
10	35	22	9	14	17
17	22	24	24	16	24
21	11	22	13	22	22

MIND OVER MATTER

82 Given that the letters are valued 1-26 according to their respective places in the alphabet, can you crack the mystery code to reveal the missing letter?

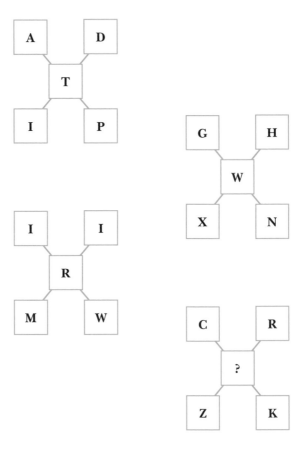

DOMINOLOGICAL

A set of dominoes is to be placed in four rows as shown below. The numbers indicate which values are shown on all the dominoes in each column and the relevant half of the domino in every row. Find out where each domino is placed by carefully comparing rows and columns to determine the possible positions of certain dominoes: for instance, if any column contains only one 6, then the domino 6/6 isn't in that column.

83

A set of dominoes consists of:

0/0, 0/1, 0/2, 0/3, 0/4, 0/5, 0/6, 1/1, 1/2, 1/3, 1/4, 1/5, 1/6,
2/2, 2/3, 2/4, 2/5, 2/6, 3/3, 3/4, 3/5, 3/6, 4/4, 4/5, 4/6, 5/5, 5/6, 6/6.

	1, 3, 3, 3, 4, 4, 5, 5.	0, 0, 1, 2, 2, 2, 6, 6.	1, 3, 4, 4, 5, 5, 5, 6.	1, 2, 2, 2, 4, 6, 6, 6.	0, 0, 1, 1, 3, 3, 3, 5.	0, 0, 0, 1, 4, 5, 6, 6.	0, 1, 2, 2, 3, 4, 4, 5.
1, 2, 2, 3, 4, 4, 5.	3						
0, 0, 1, 2, 2, 4, 5.	1						
0, 1, 3, 5, 6, 6, 6.							
0, 3, 4, 4, 4, 5, 6.							
0, 1, 2, 2, 3, 5, 5.							
0, 0, 0, 3, 4, 5, 6.							
1, 1, 2, 2, 4, 5, 6.							
1, 1, 3, 3, 3, 6, 6.							

TILE TWISTER

84 Place the eight tiles into the puzzle grid so that all adjacent numbers on each tile match up. Tiles may be rotated through 360 degrees, but none may be flipped over.

4	4
2	3

2	2
4	1

3	1
2	4

4	1
1	2

4	2
2	1

1	2
2	1

1	2
2	3

2	4
1	1

1	3				
3	4				

PIECEWORK

Place all twelve of the pieces into the grid. Any may be rotated or flipped over, but none may touch another, not even diagonally. The numbers outside the grid refer to the number of consecutive black squares; and each block is separated from the others by at least one white square. For instance, '3 2' could refer to a row with none, one or more white squares, then three black squares, then at least one white square, then two more black squares, followed by any number of white squares.

			3	1			3	1			
			1	1		1	2	1	1		
		1	3	2	3	1	1	2	4	2	2
		2	1	2	2	1	3	1	2	1	4	5

	1	2										
3	2	2										
1	1	3										
		1										
1	2	1										
3	1	1										
1	1	1										
3	1	1										
1	1	1										
	1	2										
	2	2										
1	1	1										
	1	1										
3	1	2										
1	3	1										

NUMBER FILL

86 With the starters already given, can you fit all of the remaining listed numbers into this grid? Take care, this puzzle may not be as easy as it looks!

26	190	628	8990	34030	79088
33	278	708	9871	41265	85390
60	347	780	10183	47290	85653
66	390	874	13062	49495	90456
73	402	914	15270	54003	95279
85	465	943	19701	54909	99898
90	467 ✓	1057	26820	56951	422431
94	507	2246	27596	63365	502730
143	544	3556	30430	68238	763889
180	627	7250	33276	78067	832569

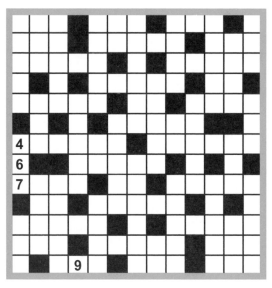

PYRAMID PLUS

Every brick in this pyramid contains a number which is the sum of the two numbers below it, so that F=A+B, etc. Just work out the missing numbers!

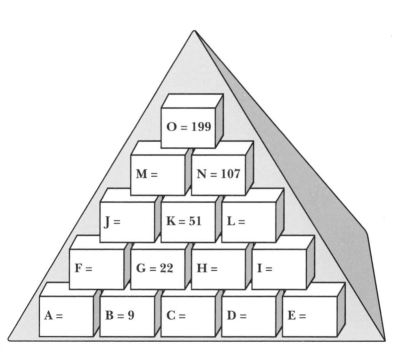

TREASURE HUNT

88 The chart gives directions to a hidden treasure behind the centre black square in the grid. Move the indicated number of spaces north, south, east and west (eg 4N means move four squares north) stopping at every square once only to arrive there. At which square should you start?

N

3E	1E	2E	2W	2S
1N	3E	1E	1S	2W
1N	1E	■	2W	2S
1N	1E	1S	2W	1W
1N	3N	1W	3W	1N

W ⇐   ⇒ E

S

FUTOSHIKI

Fill the grid so that every horizontal row and vertical column contains the numbers 1-5. The 'greater than' or 'less than' signs indicate where a number is larger or smaller than that in the neighbouring square.

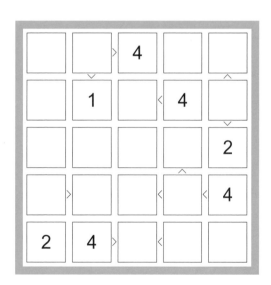

SPIDOKU

90 Each of the eight segments of the spider's web should be filled with a different number from 1 to 8, in such a way that every ring also contains a different number from 1 to 8. The segments run from the outside of the spider's web to the centre, and the rings run all the way around. Some numbers are already in place. Can you fill in the rest?

LETTER LOCATOR

Every oval shape in this diagram contains a different letter of the
alphabet from A to K inclusive. Use the clues to determine their
locations. Reference in the clues to 'due' means in any location along
the same horizontal or vertical line.

1 The B is due north of the K, which is due east of the F.

2 The C is due south of the E.

3 The D is due south of the A, which is due west of the H.

4 The E is due east of the J, and due south of the H.

5 The G is due north of the I, and due west of the A.

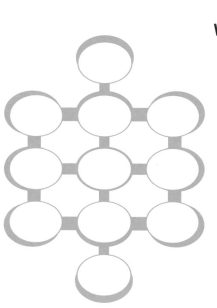

SUM CIRCLE

92 Fill the three empty circles with the symbols +, – and x in some order, to make a sum which totals the number in the centre. Each symbol must be used once and calculations are made in the direction of travel (clockwise).

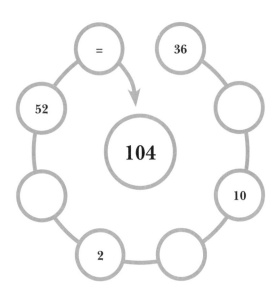

ONE TO NINE

Using the numbers below, complete these six equations (three reading across and three reading downwards). Every number is used once.

93

2	**3**	**4**	
6	**7**	**8**	**9**

	+		x	5	=	85
−	■	x	■	x		
	÷		+		=	7
x	■	−	■	+		
	+	1	x		=	28
=		=		=		
9		15		27		

WORK IT OUT

94 In the grid below, which number should replace the question mark?

12	15	3	9	21	6	18
30	20	25	5	10	35	15
42	12	24	6	18	36	30
28	16	12	4	8	20	24
6	12	14	2	8	4	10
14	49	35	28	7	21	42
32	16	40	48	?	56	8

Each symbol stands for a different number. In order to reach the correct total at the end of each row and column, what is the value of the circle, cross, pentagon, square and star?

95

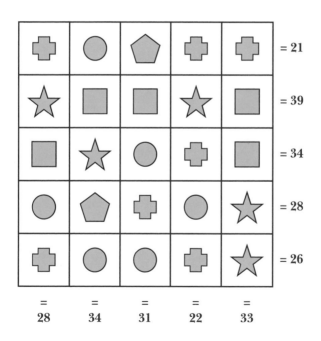

Logi-6

96

Every row and column of this grid should contain one each of the numbers 1, 2, 3, 4, 5 and 6. Each of the six shapes (marked by thicker lines) should also contain one each of the numbers 1, 2, 3, 4, 5 and 6. Can you complete the grid?

	1				
4		5	6		
			1		3
		1	2		
	6	2		4	

DOMINO PLACEMENT

A standard set of 28 dominoes has been laid out as shown. Can you draw in the edges of them all? The check-box is provided as an aid and the domino already placed will help.

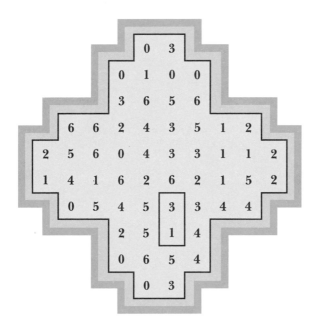

0-0	0-1	0-2	0-3	0-4	0-5	0-6	1-1	1-2	1-3	1-4	1-5	1-6	2-2
									✓				

2-3	2-4	2-5	2-6	3-3	3-4	3-5	3-6	4-4	4-5	4-6	5-5	5-6	6-6

98

Which four pieces can be fitted together to form an exact copy of this shape?

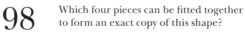

A

B

D

C

E

F

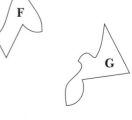
G

H

I

J

SHAPE UP

Every row and column in this grid originally contained one heart, one club, one diamond, one spade and two blank squares, although not necessarily in that order.

99

Every symbol with a black arrow refers to the first of the four symbols encountered when travelling in the direction of the arrow. Every symbol with a white arrow refers to the second of the four symbols encountered in the direction of the arrow.

Can you complete the original grid?

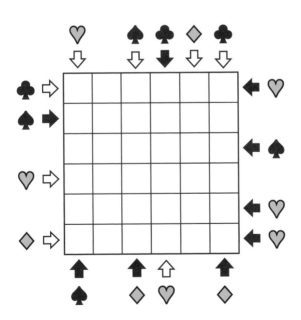

100

The blank squares below should be filled with whole numbers between 1 and 30 inclusive, any of which may occur more than once, or not at all.

The numbers in every horizontal row add up to the totals on the right, as do the two long diagonal lines; whilst those in every vertical column add up to the totals along the bottom.

							116

17	5			21	8	20	93
3		13	16	19		22	97
23	1	9	4		7	8	66
30		15		23	10	18	124
	29	27	6	7	18		123
22	9	11	16	11		17	107
12	28		26		25	6	121
119	90	91	103	105	108	115	80

COMPARISONS

Look at figures A and B, comparing the two, then try to discover which of the three alternatives (D, E or F) most closely follows the pattern in relation to C.

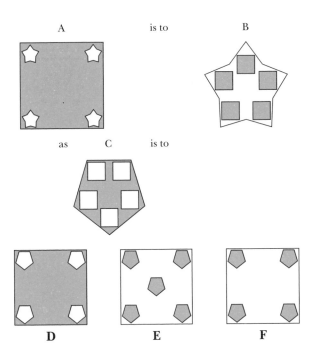

A   is to   B

as   C   is to

D   E   F

HEXAGONY

102 Can you place the hexagons into the grid, so that where any hexagon touches another along a straight line, the number in both triangles is the same? No rotation of any hexagon is allowed!

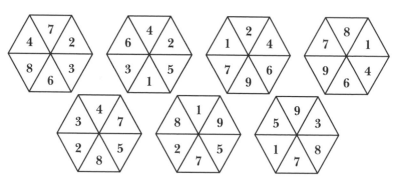

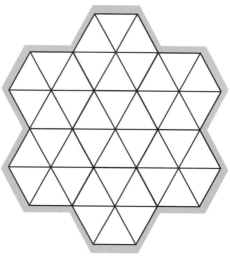

Ls in Place

Twelve L-shapes like the ones here need to be inserted in the grid and each L has one hole in it.

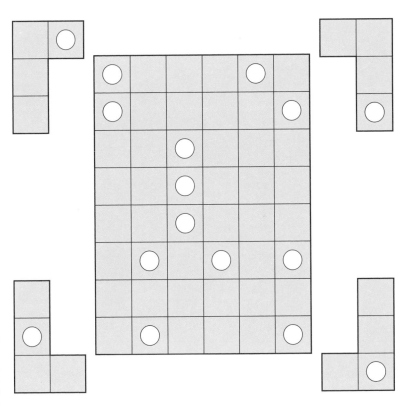

103

There are three pieces of each of the four kinds shown here and any piece may be turned or flipped over before being put in the grid. No pieces of the same kind may touch, even at a corner.

The pieces fit together so well that you cannot see any spaces between them; only the holes show.

Can you tell where the Ls are?

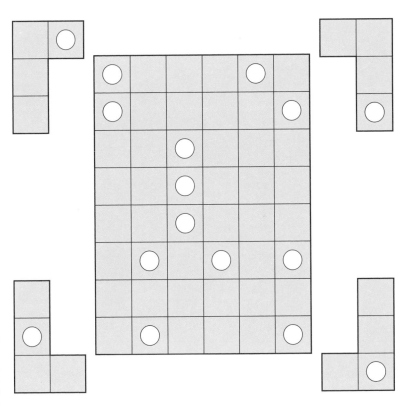

104

In this puzzle, an amateur coin collector has been out with his metal detector, searching for booty. He didn't have time to dig up all the coins he found, so he made a grid map, showing their locations, in the hope that if he loses the map, at least no-one else will be able to understand it…

Those squares containing numbers are empty, but where a number appears in a square, it indicates how many coins are located in the squares (up to a maximum of eight) surrounding the numbered one, touching it at any corner or side. There is only one coin in any individual square.

Place a circle into every square containing a coin.

1								1	
	3	5			1		0		
1	2					1		2	
1				5				2	1
	2				1				
	3							1	
	4	4			2	3			1
	4					4		3	
			3						2
	2	1	2	2	4			1	

Latin Square

The grid should be filled with numbers from 1 to 6, so that each number appears just once in every row and column. The clues refer to the digit totals in the squares, eg A 1 2 3 = 6 means that the numbers in squares A1, A2 and A3 add up to 6.

105

1 F 1 2 3 = 14

2 C D E 1 = 10

3 A 4 5 = 6

4 E 3 4 = 4

5 D 4 5 6 = 9

6 D 2 3 = 11

7 A B C 2 = 6

8 B C 3 = 8

9 C 3 4 5 = 9

10 E F 6 = 3

11 B C D 5 = 8

12 A B 6 = 10

	A	B	C	D	E	F
1						
2						
3						
4						
5						
6						

SIMPLE AS A, B, C?

106 Each of the small squares in the grid below contains either A, B or C. Every row and column has exactly two of each letter, as do the two long diagonal lines of six squares. Can you tell the letter in each square?

Across

1 The Bs are further right than the Cs.

2 The As are between the Bs.

4 The Bs are further left than the Cs.

6 The Bs are between the Cs.

Down

1 The As are between the Bs.

2 The Cs are between the As.

3 The Bs are between the Cs.

4 The Cs are higher than the As.

5 The As are higher than the Bs.

	1	2	3	4	5	6
1						
2						
3						
4						
5						
6						

ZIGZAG

The object of this puzzle is to trace a single path from the top left corner to the bottom right corner of the grid, travelling through all of the cells in either a horizontal, vertical or diagonal direction.

107

Every cell must be entered once only and your path should take you through the numbers in the sequence 1-2-3-4-5-6-1-2-3-4-5-6, etc.

Can you find the way?

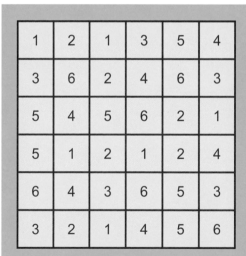

1	2	1	3	5	4
3	6	2	4	6	3
5	4	5	6	2	1
5	1	2	1	2	4
6	4	3	6	5	3
3	2	1	4	5	6

113

BATTLESHIPS

108 Can you place the vessels into the diagram? Some parts of vessels or sea squares have already been filled in. A number to the right or below a row or column refers to the number of occupied squares in that row or column.

Any vessel may be positioned horizontally or vertically, but no part of a vessel touches part of any other vessel, either horizontally, vertically or diagonally.

Empty Area of Sea: ≈

Aircraft Carrier: ◀■■▶

Battleships: ◀■▶ ◀■▶

Cruisers: ◀▸ ◀▸ ◀▸

Submarines: ● ● ● ●

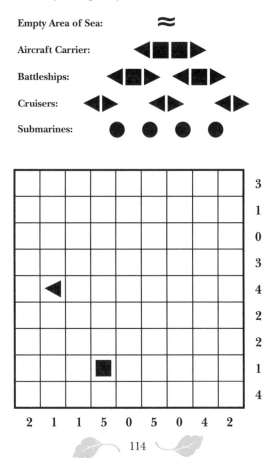

3
1
0
3
4
2
2
1
4

2 1 1 5 0 5 0 4 2

THE BOTTOM LINE

Can you fill each square in the bottom line with the correct digit?
Every square in the solution contains only one digit from the lines
above, although two or more squares in the solution may contain the
same digit.

109

At the end of every row is a score, which shows:

a the number of digits placed in the correct finishing
   position on the bottom line, as indicated by a tick; and

b the number of digits which appear on the bottom line,
   but in a different position, as indicated by a cross.

SCORE

2	4	1	8	✔ ✗
5	3	2	7	✔
2	8	4	5	✗ ✗
4	7	2	6	✔ ✔
4	6	1	2	✔ ✔
				✔ ✔ ✔ ✔

110

Draw a single continuous loop, by connecting the dots. No line may cross the path of another.

The figure inside each set of any four surrounding dots indicates the total number of surrounding lines.

```
2       2 3 2       3
3 0     1 2 0       0
3 1 2     3         2 1
    2 1         2   2 2
1 2 1 2 1 1 3 1     2
2 2     2 1       1 2 1
    2     0 2 1       2
    2 0 1             2
2             1 2 1
2 0 2 2 1 2         3
  1     1 0 2     1 1
  2 2 3       3     2
```

COMBIKU

Each horizontal row and vertical column should contain different shapes and different numbers.

Every square will contain one number and one shape and no combination may be repeated anywhere else in the puzzle.

111

112 In the diagram below, which number should replace the question mark?

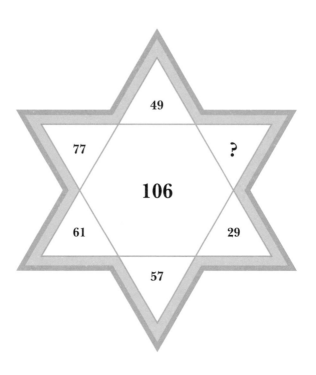

ADDING UP

In the square below, change the positions of six numbers, one per horizontal row, vertical column and long diagonal line of six smaller squares, in such a way that the numbers in each row, column and long diagonal line total exactly 137. Any number may appear more than once in a row, column or line.

16	5	17	37	54	10
38	22	14	10	27	23
24	37	22	20	24	20
21	37	27	9	5	23
8	26	30	36	13	23
29	17	24	10	24	40

114 Given that the letters are valued 1-26 according to their respective places in the alphabet, can you crack the mystery code to reveal the missing letter?

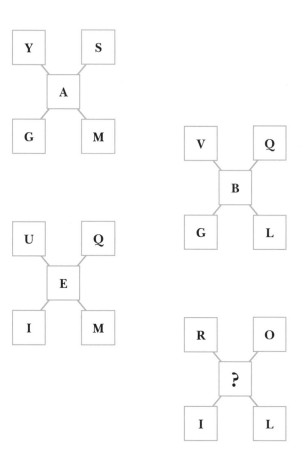

Which of the four lettered alternatives (A, B, C or D) fits most logically into the empty square?

115

8	11	3
7	15	9
12	26	6

18	15	10
7	3	19
8	6	11

4	2	11
10	22	8
18	17	5

?

14	19	9
21	16	10
5	12	3

A

1	2	3
13	14	25
17	12	10

B

1	10	9
14	2	21
12	13	17

C

25	14	10
15	3	4
9	6	12

D

TILE TWISTER

116

Place the eight tiles into the puzzle grid so that all adjacent numbers on each tile match up. Tiles may be rotated through 360 degrees, but none may be flipped over.

4	4
2	1

4	1
1	2

3	1
2	1

3	2
2	4

3	2
1	3

3	3
1	2

4	1
4	1

4	3
1	3

				3	4
				2	3

Piecework

117

Place all twelve of the pieces into the grid. Any may be rotated or flipped over, but none may touch another, not even diagonally. The numbers outside the grid refer to the number of consecutive black squares; and each block is separated from the others by at least one white square. For instance, '3 2' could refer to a row with none, one or more white squares, then three black squares, then at least one white square, then two more black squares, followed by any number of white squares.

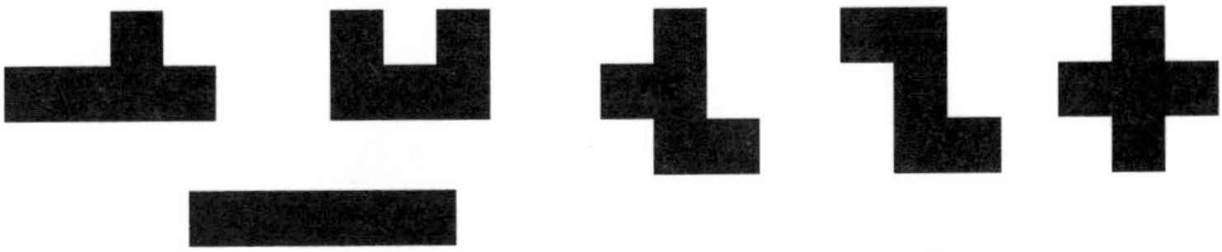

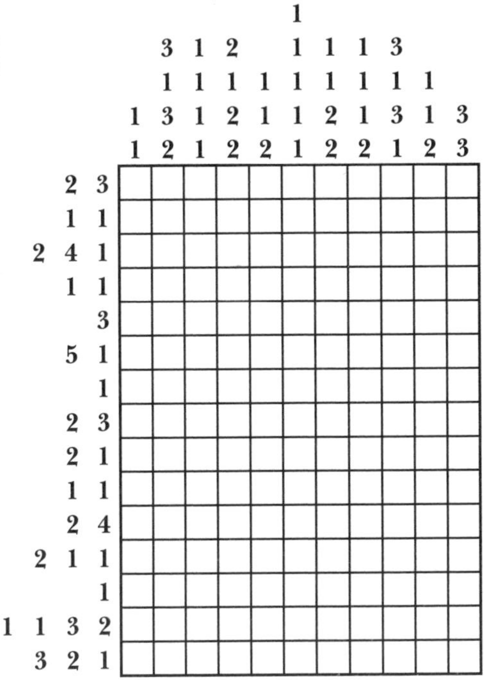
1 1
3 1 3 2
1 1 1 1
2 1 2 2
1 1 2
1 1 1 1 1
1 1 2 2
1 1 1 2
3 1 3 1
1 1 2
3 3
2 3
1 1
2 4 1
1 1
3
5 1
1
2 3
2 1
1 1
2 4
2 1 1
1
1 1 3 2
3 2 1

NUMBER FILL

118

With the starter already given, can you fit all of the remaining listed numbers into this grid? Take care, this puzzle may not be as easy as it looks!

14	258	603	2480	9870	73097
20	263	650	2768	9883	76099
23	301	719	2889	24724	76852
36	346	780	3056	31567	80047
44	349	790	4365	36873	96456
45	432	815	4579	37962	99531
145	455	840	5567	38059	267733
191	495	900	7094	56279	404940
196	541	925	8691	61120	452512
207	547	956	8707 ✓	65900	832144

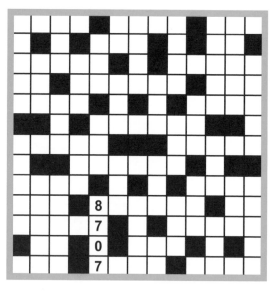

PYRAMID PLUS

Every brick in this pyramid contains a number which is the sum of the two numbers below it, so that F=A+B, etc. Just work out the missing numbers!

119

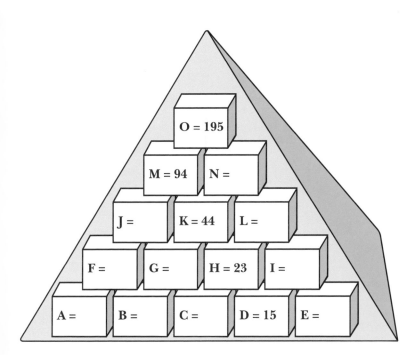

O = 195

M = 94   N =

J =   K = 44   L =

F =   G =   H = 23   I =

A =   B =   C =   D = 15   E =

TREASURE HUNT

120 The chart gives directions to a hidden treasure behind the centre black square in the grid. Move the indicated number of spaces north, south, east and west (eg 4N means move four squares north) stopping at every square once only to arrive there. At which square should you start?

N

↑

1S	1W	1E	1E	1S
2E	3S	1E	2W	3S
2E	1S	■	3W	3W
3E	3N	3N	1E	2W
1N	1E	1E	2N	2N

W ⇐   ⇒ E

⇩

S

FUTOSHIKI

Fill the grid so that every horizontal row and vertical column contains the numbers 1-5. The 'greater than' or 'less than' signs indicate where a number is larger or smaller than that in the neighbouring square.

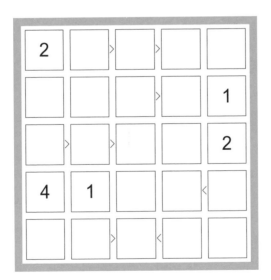

122

Each of the eight segments of the spider's web should be filled with a different number from 1 to 8, in such a way that every ring also contains a different number from 1 to 8. The segments run from the outside of the spider's web to the centre, and the rings run all the way around. Some numbers are already in place. Can you fill in the rest?

LETTER LOCATOR

Every oval shape in this diagram contains a different letter of the
alphabet from A to K inclusive. Use the clues to determine their
locations. Reference in the clues to 'due' means in any location along
the same horizontal or vertical line.

1 The A is next to and due south of the
   J, which is due east of the H.

2 The F is further south than the C, further east
   than the J, and further north than the D.

3 The H is due north of the E, which is
   next to and due west of the G.

4 The J is further north than the B,
   which is due west of the K.

5 The K is due south of the I.

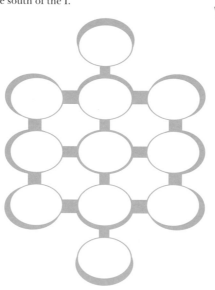

SUM CIRCLE

124

Fill the three empty circles with the symbols +, – and x in some order, to make a sum which totals the number in the centre. Each symbol must be used once and calculations are made in the direction of travel (clockwise).

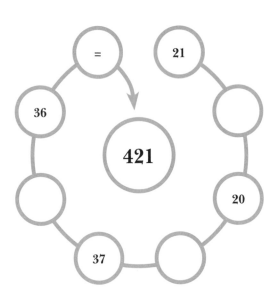

ONE TO NINE

Using the numbers below, complete these six equations (three reading across and three reading downwards). Every number is used once.

125

```
    1       4       5
6       7       8       9
```

	x		+		=	25
x	■	x	■	x		
	x		+	2	=	65
−	■	−	■	x		
	+	3	+		=	16
=		=		=		
20		51		10		

131

WORK IT OUT

126 In the grid below, which two-digit number should replace the question mark?

8	24	17	21	19	99	10
16	12	87	29	7	14	9
27	88	3	17	20	16	5
6	13	14	27	6	34	100
79	1	22	4	11	31	10
113	28	19	2	7	18	39
10	?	23	94	12	30	7

Symbol Sums

Each symbol stands for a different number. In order to reach the correct total at the end of each row and column, what is the value of the circle, cross, pentagon, square and star?

127

○	✚	○	⬠	◻	= 14
★	★	○	○	★	= 11
◻	★	✚	○	★	= 13
✚	⬠	○	○	◻	= 14
○	○	⬠	⬠	○	= 15
=11	=17	=13	=15	=11	

LOGI-6

128 Every row and column of this grid should contain one each of the numbers 1, 2, 3, 4, 5 and 6. Each of the six shapes (marked by thicker lines) should also contain one each of the numbers 1, 2, 3, 4, 5 and 6. Can you complete the grid?

				2	
3					
	4	3	5		
5	1	6			
1			4		

A standard set of 28 dominoes has been laid out as shown. Can you draw in the edges of them all? The check-box is provided as an aid and the domino already placed will help.

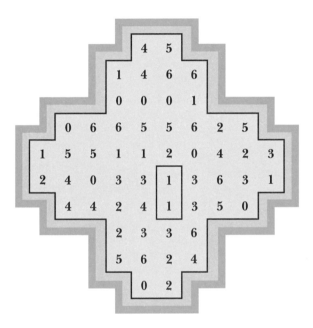

0-0	0-1	0-2	0-3	0-4	0-5	0-6	1-1	1-2	1-3	1-4	1-5	1-6	2-2
							✔						

2-3	2-4	2-5	2-6	3-3	3-4	3-5	3-6	4-4	4-5	4-6	5-5	5-6	6-6

BALANCING THE SCALES

130 Given that scales A and B balance perfectly, how many hearts are needed to balance scale C?

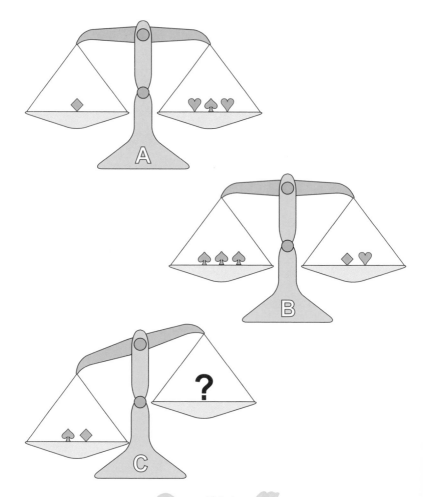

SHAPE UP

Every row and column in this grid originally contained one heart, one club, one diamond, one spade and two blank squares, although not necessarily in that order.

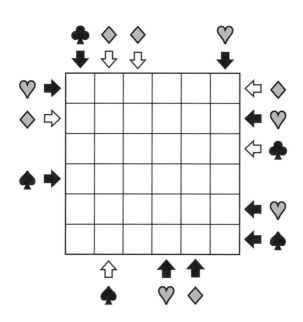

Every symbol with a black arrow refers to the first of the four symbols encountered when travelling in the direction of the arrow. Every symbol with a white arrow refers to the second of the four symbols encountered in the direction of the arrow.

Can you complete the original grid?

TOTAL CONCENTRATION

132

The blank squares below should be filled with whole numbers between 1 and 30 inclusive, any of which may occur more than once, or not at all.

The numbers in every horizontal row add up to the totals on the right, as do the two long diagonal lines; whilst those in every vertical column add up to the totals along the bottom.

							103

	8	2	12	26	28		117
1		25		11	9	15	90
17	1		6	3		29	89
5	30	18		30	10	21	138
29	23		9		27	7	125
22	4	3	28		24	21	121
	4	6	2		10	20	61

99	83	105	97	102	115	140	126

WHATEVER NEXT?

Draw in the missing hands on the final clock.

133

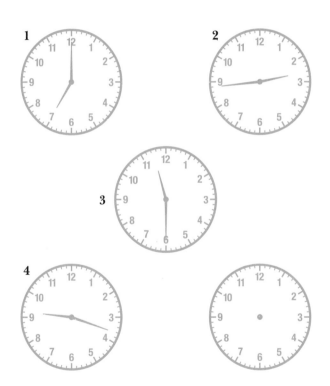

1

2

3

4

HEXAGONY

134
Can you place the hexagons into the grid, so that where any hexagon touches another along a straight line, the number in both triangles is the same? No rotation of any hexagon is allowed!

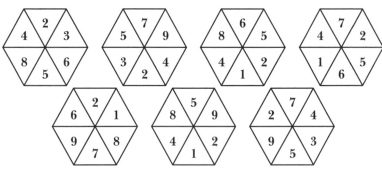

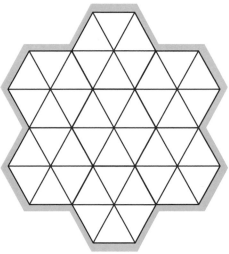

Ls in Place

Twelve L-shapes like the ones here need to be inserted in the grid and each L has one hole in it.

There are three pieces of each of the four kinds shown here and any piece may be turned or flipped over before being put in the grid. No pieces of the same kind may touch, even at a corner.

The pieces fit together so well that you cannot see any spaces between them; only the holes show.

Can you tell where the Ls are?

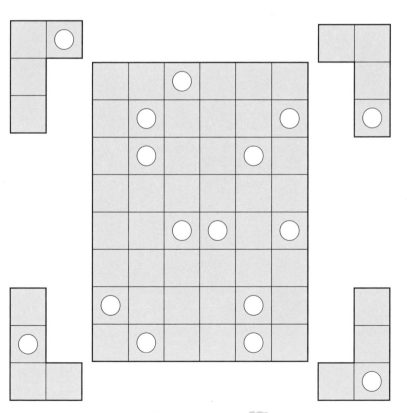

COIN COLLECTING

136

In this puzzle, an amateur coin collector has been out with his metal detector, searching for booty. He didn't have time to dig up all the coins he found, so he made a grid map, showing their locations, in the hope that if he loses the map, at least no-one else will be able to understand it…

Those squares containing numbers are empty, but where a number appears in a square, it indicates how many coins are located in the squares (up to a maximum of eight) surrounding the numbered one, touching it at any corner or side. There is only one coin in any individual square.

Place a circle into every square containing a coin.

1		1					2	2	2
	1				1	1			
	0					1			
		1		0	1			4	
1		2						3	2
1			3		3				
		2				3	4		
	3		3		2				1
3			2	1		4			1
		2						0	

LATIN SQUARE

The grid should be filled with numbers from 1 to 6, so that each number appears just once in every row and column. The clues refer to the digit totals in the squares, eg A 1 2 3 = 6 means that the numbers in squares A1, A2 and A3 add up to 6.

137

1	D E 3 = 6	7	B C 5 = 5
2	B 1 2 = 6	8	C D 6 = 9
3	F 4 5 = 8	9	C 3 4 = 3
4	A 3 4 5 = 12	10	E F 5 = 11
5	D E F 2 = 6	11	D E 4 = 10
6	E 1 2 3 = 8	12	B 5 6 = 6

	A	B	C	D	E	F
1						
2						
3						
4						
5						
6						

Simple as A, B, C?

138

Each of the small squares in the grid below contains either A, B or C. Every row and column has exactly two of each letter, as do the two long diagonal lines of six squares. Can you tell the letter in each square?

Across

3 The Cs are between the As.
4 The Cs are between the As.

Down

1 The Bs are between the Cs.
2 The As are between the Bs.
3 The As are between the Bs.
4 The Bs are between the Cs.
5 The As are between the Bs.
6 The As are between the Bs.

	1	2	3	4	5	6
1						
2						
3						
4						
5						
6						

ZIGZAG

The object of this puzzle is to trace a single path from the top left corner to the bottom right corner of the grid, travelling through all of the cells in either a horizontal, vertical or diagonal direction.

Every cell must be entered once only and your path should take you through the numbers in the sequence 1-2-3-4-5-6-1-2-3-4-5-6, etc.

Can you find the way?

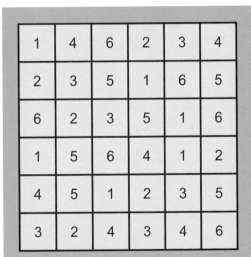

1	4	6	2	3	4
2	3	5	1	6	5
6	2	3	5	1	6
1	5	6	4	1	2
4	5	1	2	3	5
3	2	4	3	4	6

140

Can you place the vessels into the diagram? Some parts of vessels or sea squares have already been filled in. A number to the right or below a row or column refers to the number of occupied squares in that row or column.

Any vessel may be positioned horizontally or vertically, but no part of a vessel touches part of any other vessel, either horizontally, vertically or diagonally.

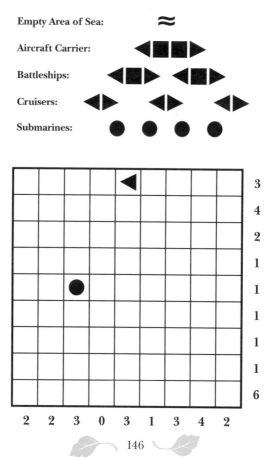

Empty Area of Sea:	≈
Aircraft Carrier:	◀■■▶
Battleships:	◀■▶ ◀■▶
Cruisers:	◀▶ ◀▶ ◀▶
Submarines:	● ● ● ●

The grid has the following clues:

Rows (top to bottom): 3, 4, 2, 1, 1, 1, 1, 1, 6

Columns (left to right): 2, 2, 3, 0, 3, 1, 3, 4, 2

THE BOTTOM LINE

Can you fill each square in the bottom line with the correct digit?
Every square in the solution contains only one digit from the lines
above, although two or more squares in the solution may contain the
same digit.

141

At the end of every row is a score, which shows:

  a the number of digits placed in the correct finishing
       position on the bottom line, as indicated by a tick; and

  b the number of digits which appear on the bottom line,
       but in a different position, as indicated by a cross.

SCORE

2	8	1	1	✗
8	7	6	3	✗ ✗
6	9	2	4	✗
4	1	3	7	✗
4	4	9	9	✗
				✓✓✓✓

SLITHERLINK

142 Draw a single continuous loop, by connecting the dots. No line may cross the path of another.

The figure inside each set of any four surrounding dots indicates the total number of surrounding lines.

```
3       3 2       2 1 2
2 2     0     1     3 1 2
1 3         2     2 2 1
  1 1 2 0 2
2 1                 3 2 3
          1     2 1 1
          2 1             1
2 1     1 2       2 2
3     2 2 1     1 2 2
  1 0 2       1       3 1
2         0 1 2 2     1 3
  1 2     2 2 2 2
```

COMBIKU

Each horizontal row and vertical column should contain different shapes and different numbers.

Every square will contain one number and one shape and no combination may be repeated anywhere else in the puzzle.

◇ ○ ☆ ⬡ ▢
1   2   3   4   5

◇	1	⬡		
5	4			
			◇	
		○		
	◇		2	3

144 In the diagram below, which letter should replace the question mark?

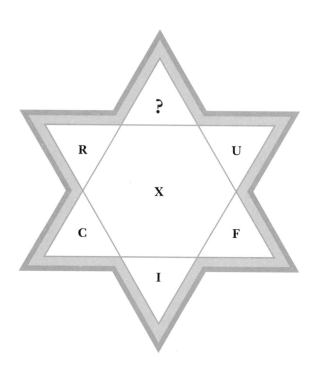

ADDING UP

In the square below, change the positions of six numbers, one per horizontal row, vertical column and long diagonal line of six smaller squares, in such a way that the numbers in each row, column and long diagonal line total exactly 143. Any number may appear more than once in a row, column or line.

145

44	8	29	26	35	18
27	23	23	14	27	28
16	35	23	19	17	26
15	32	28	12	13	28
13	29	30	30	12	28
21	23	27	27	38	14

146 Given that the letters are valued 1-26 according to their respective places in the alphabet, can you crack the mystery code to reveal the missing letter?

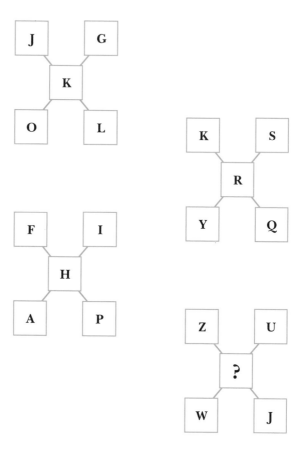

DOMINOLOGICAL

A set of dominoes is to be placed in four rows as shown below. The numbers indicate which values are shown on all the dominoes in each column and the relevant half of the domino in every row. Find out where each domino is placed by carefully comparing rows and columns to determine the possible positions of certain dominoes: for instance, if any column contains only one 6, then the domino 6/6 isn't in that column.

147

A set of dominoes consists of:

0/0, 0/1, 0/2, 0/3, 0/4, 0/5, 0/6, 1/1, 1/2, 1/3, 1/4, 1/5, 1/6, 2/2, 2/3, 2/4, 2/5, 2/6, 3/3, 3/4, 3/5, 3/6, 4/4, 4/5, 4/6, 5/5, 5/6, 6/6.

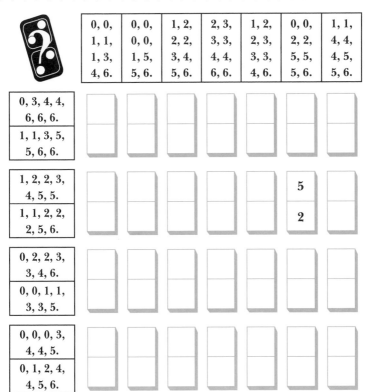

	0, 0, 1, 1, 1, 3, 4, 6.	0, 0, 0, 0, 1, 5, 5, 6.	1, 2, 2, 3, 4, 5, 6.	2, 3, 3, 3, 4, 4, 6, 6.	1, 2, 2, 3, 3, 3, 4, 6.	0, 0, 2, 2, 5, 5, 5, 6.	1, 1, 4, 4, 4, 5, 5, 6.
0, 3, 4, 4, 6, 6, 6.							
1, 1, 3, 5, 5, 6, 6.							
1, 2, 2, 3, 4, 5, 5.						5	
1, 1, 2, 2, 2, 5, 6.						2	
0, 2, 2, 3, 3, 4, 6.							
0, 0, 1, 1, 3, 3, 5.							
0, 0, 0, 3, 4, 4, 5.							
0, 1, 2, 4, 4, 5, 6.							

TILE TWISTER

148 Place the eight tiles into the puzzle grid so that all adjacent numbers on each tile match up. Tiles may be rotated through 360 degrees, but none may be flipped over.

4	1
1	4

2	3
3	1

4	1
1	2

3	1
3	2

2	3
4	1

4	4
3	1

3	2
1	1

1	3
1	1

				4	1
				2	3

Piecework

149

Place all twelve of the pieces into the grid. Any may be rotated or flipped over, but none may touch another, not even diagonally. The numbers outside the grid refer to the number of consecutive black squares; and each block is separated from the others by at least one white square. For instance, '3 2' could refer to a row with none, one or more white squares, then three black squares, then at least one white square, then two more black squares, followed by any number of white squares.

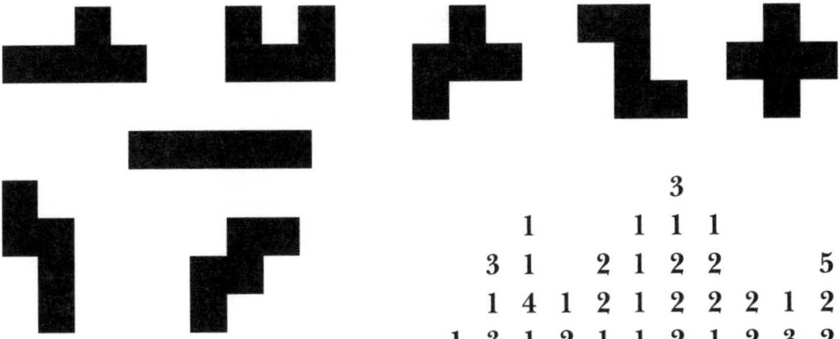

Column clues (left to right, top to bottom): 1 | 3 1 3 | 1 1 4 1 | 1 2 | 2 2 1 | 1 1 1 1 | 3 1 2 2 2 | 1 2 2 1 | 2 2 | 1 3 | 5 2 2

Row clues (top to bottom):

1 1
1 3 1
3 1 1
1 1
1 2 1
3 2 1
1
2 1 1 1
1 3 3
1 1
1 2 1
3 1
3 2
1 4 1
1 1

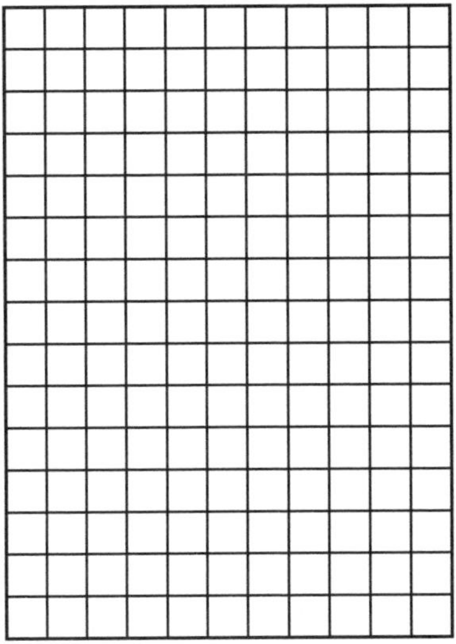

Number Fill

150 With the starter already given, can you fit all of the remaining listed numbers into this grid? Take care, this puzzle may not be as easy as it looks!

10	87	562	3233 ✓	39252	97282
11	99	634	4482	52673	97314
13	206	712	4538	55284	141421
25	213	835	7083	61309	321743
43	287	872	8434	64510	331244
47	293	980	9029	71534	429871
60	325	1217	13231	73018	493210
62	376	1709	24323	85231	545427
69	423	1863	30108	86557	616992
78	453	2224	37820	91165	978425

PYRAMID PLUS

Every brick in this pyramid contains a number which is the sum of the two numbers below it, so that F=A+B, etc. Just work out the missing numbers!

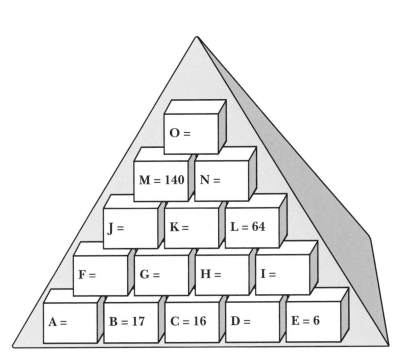

O =

M = 140   N =

J =   K =   L = 64

F =   G =   H =   I =

A =   B = 17   C = 16   D =   E = 6

TREASURE HUNT

152 The chart gives directions to a hidden treasure behind the centre black square in the grid. Move the indicated number of spaces north, south, east and west (eg 4N means move four squares north) stopping at every square once only to arrive there. At which square should you start?

N

↑

2S	1E	2E	3W	1S
1E	1N	2W	1N	1W
2S	1E	■	2W	1W
1E	1E	2E	1S	1N
1N	3E	3N	2W	2W

W ⇐   ⇒ E

⇩

S

FUTOSHIKI

Fill the grid so that every horizontal row and vertical column contains the numbers 1-5. The 'greater than' or 'less than' signs indicate where a number is larger or smaller than that in the neighbouring square.

153

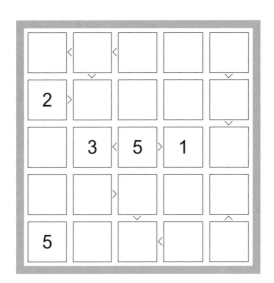

SPIDOKU

154

Each of the eight segments of the spider's web should be filled with a different number from 1 to 8, in such a way that every ring also contains a different number from 1 to 8. The segments run from the outside of the spider's web to the centre, and the rings run all the way around. Some numbers are already in place. Can you fill in the rest?

LETTER LOCATOR

Every oval shape in this diagram contains a different letter of the
alphabet from A to K inclusive. Use the clues to determine their
locations. Reference in the clues to 'due' means in any location along
the same horizontal or vertical line.

1   The A is next to and due south of the D.

2   The C is due south of the E.

3   The D is due east of the H, which is due south of the K.

4   The E is further east than the H, which
    is further north than the G.

5   The F is next to and due south of the
    G, which is due east of the B.

6   The J is due east of the I, which is next
    to and due south of the E.

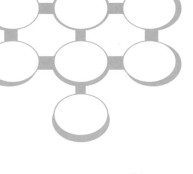

156

Fill the three empty circles with the symbols +, – and x in some order, to make a sum which totals the number in the centre. Each symbol must be used once and calculations are made in the direction of travel (clockwise).

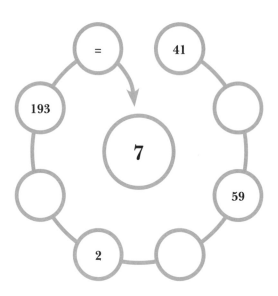

ONE TO NINE

Using the numbers below, complete these six equations (three reading across and three reading downwards). Every number is used once.

1   2   3
5   6   7   9

	x		+	8	=	23
x	■	x	■	x		
	x		x		=	84
+	■	+	■	+		
	x	4	x		=	36
=		=		=		
7		34		65		

WORK IT OUT

158 In the grid below, which number should replace the question mark?

4	3	12	1	12	2	24
6	8	48	2	96	3	288
2	11	22	3	66	1	66
7	6	42	4	168	1	168
10	1	10	2	?	4	80
3	4	12	8	96	2	192
9	3	27	2	54	3	162

SYMBOL SUMS

Each symbol stands for a different number. In order to reach the correct total at the end of each row and column, what is the value of the circle, cross, pentagon, square and star?

159

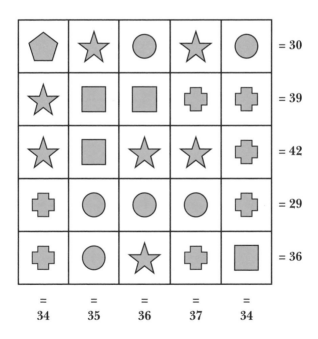

Logi-6

160 Every row and column of this grid should contain one each of the numbers 1, 2, 3, 4, 5 and 6. Each of the six shapes (marked by thicker lines) should also contain one each of the numbers 1, 2, 3, 4, 5 and 6. Can you complete the grid?

	2				6
5	3		6		1
2	6		3		
	5	4	2		
					2
	1				

DOMINO PLACEMENT

A standard set of 28 dominoes has been laid out as shown. Can you draw in the edges of them all? The check-box is provided as an aid and the domino already placed will help.

0-0	0-1	0-2	0-3	0-4	0-5	0-6	1-1	1-2	1-3	1-4	1-5	1-6	2-2
								✔					

2-3	2-4	2-5	2-6	3-3	3-4	3-5	3-6	4-4	4-5	4-6	5-5	5-6	6-6

JIGSAW

162

Which four pieces can be fitted together to form an exact copy of this shape?

A

B

D

C

E

F

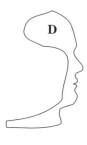

G

H

I

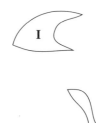
J

SHAPE UP

Every row and column in this grid originally contained one heart, one club, one diamond, one spade and two blank squares, although not necessarily in that order.

Every symbol with a black arrow refers to the first of the four symbols encountered when travelling in the direction of the arrow. Every symbol with a white arrow refers to the second of the four symbols encountered in the direction of the arrow.

Can you complete the original grid?

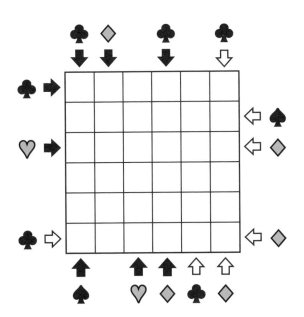

TOTAL CONCENTRATION

164

The blank squares below should be filled with whole numbers between 1 and 30 inclusive, any of which may occur more than once, or not at all.

The numbers in every horizontal row add up to the totals on the right, as do the two long diagonal lines; whilst those in every vertical column add up to the totals along the bottom.

							114
30		9	22		11	23	131
24		28	10	2		6	99
2	27	18	10		11		100
3	8	3		9		27	64
	17	6	19	1	5		77
7	30		14	26	28	4	121
13	14	16		5	15	15	107
104	133	92	105	70	104	91	101

COMPARISONS

Look at figures A and B, comparing the two, then try to discover which of the three alternatives (D, E or F) most closely follows the pattern in relation to C.

165

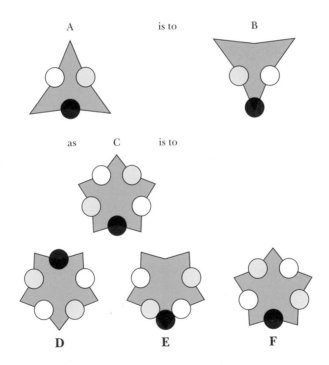

A   is to   B

as   C   is to

D   E   F

HEXAGONY

166

Can you place the hexagons into the grid, so that where any hexagon touches another along a straight line, the number in both triangles is the same? No rotation of any hexagon is allowed!

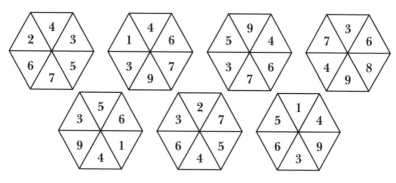

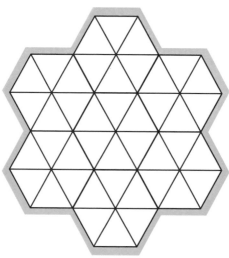

Ls in Place

Twelve L-shapes like the ones here need to be inserted in the grid and each L has one hole in it.

There are three pieces of each of the four kinds shown here and any piece may be turned or flipped over before being put in the grid. No pieces of the same kind may touch, even at a corner.

The pieces fit together so well that you cannot see any spaces between them; only the holes show.

Can you tell where the Ls are?

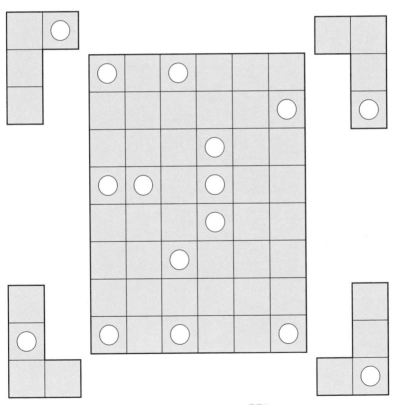

COIN COLLECTING

168

In this puzzle, an amateur coin collector has been out with his metal detector, searching for booty. He didn't have time to dig up all the coins he found, so he made a grid map, showing their locations, in the hope that if he loses the map, at least no-one else will be able to understand it…

Those squares containing numbers are empty, but where a number appears in a square, it indicates how many coins are located in the squares (up to a maximum of eight) surrounding the numbered one, touching it at any corner or side. There is only one coin in any individual square.

Place a circle into every square containing a coin.

	1		0			3	3		
	2	1						4	
	3		4			4			
						1			1
	3		2	3	2		3	3	2
1					0				
		1	1			2			1
	0			1				1	
0			2	1		2	2		1
				0					

Latin Square

The grid should be filled with numbers from 1 to 6, so that each number appears just once in every row and column. The clues refer to the digit totals in the squares, eg A 1 2 3 = 6 means that the numbers in squares A1, A2 and A3 add up to 6.

1 B C D 6 = 9

2 D 3 4 = 4

3 A B C 2 = 12

4 F 4 5 6 = 11

5 A B 4 = 10

6 B C 5 = 11

7 C D E 4 = 8

8 B C 1 = 3

9 C 5 6 = 9

10 B 3 4 5 = 11

11 E F 2 = 3

12 C 3 4 = 8

	A	B	C	D	E	F
1						
2						
3						
4						
5						
6						

SIMPLE AS **A, B, C?**

170

Each of the small squares in the grid below contains either A, B or C. Every row and column has exactly two of each letter, as do the two long diagonal lines of six squares. Can you tell the letter in each square?

Across

1 The As are further right than the Cs.
2 The As are between the Cs.
4 Each A is directly next to and left of a C.
5 The Bs are further left than the Cs.
6 The As are between the Cs.

Down

1 The As are lower than the Bs.
3 The Bs are between the As.
4 The As are between the Bs.
5 No two adjacent squares contain the same letter.
6 The As are higher than the Bs.

	1	2	3	4	5	6
1						
2						
3						
4						
5						
6						

Zigzag

The object of this puzzle is to trace a single path from the top left corner to the bottom right corner of the grid, travelling through all of the cells in either a horizontal, vertical or diagonal direction.

Every cell must be entered once only and your path should take you through the numbers in the sequence 1-2-3-4-5-6-1-2-3-4-5-6, etc.

Can you find the way?

1	2	4	5	4	3
2	3	5	6	2	1
3	1	6	1	2	6
4	5	3	4	5	3
2	6	2	1	5	4
1	3	4	5	6	6

BATTLESHIPS

172

Can you place the vessels into the diagram? Some parts of vessels or sea squares have already been filled in. A number to the right or below a row or column refers to the number of occupied squares in that row or column.

Any vessel may be positioned horizontally or vertically, but no part of a vessel touches part of any other vessel, either horizontally, vertically or diagonally.

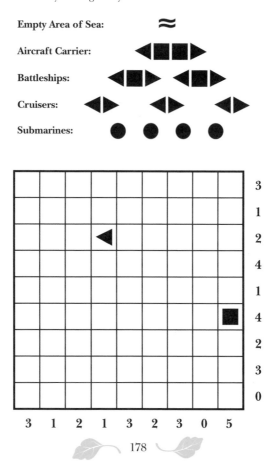

Empty Area of Sea:

Aircraft Carrier:

Battleships:

Cruisers:

Submarines:

3
1
2
4
1
4
2
3
0

3 1 2 1 3 2 3 0 5

THE BOTTOM LINE

Can you fill each square in the bottom line with the correct digit?
Every square in the solution contains only one digit from the lines
above, although two or more squares in the solution may contain the
same digit.

173

At the end of every row is a score, which shows:

a the number of digits placed in the correct finishing
position on the bottom line, as indicated by a tick; and

b the number of digits which appear on the bottom line,
but in a different position, as indicated by a cross.

SCORE

2	5	8	3	✓ ✗
4	7	8	6	✗ ✗
8	1	7	3	✗ ✗
1	3	2	7	✗ ✗
5	8	6	1	✗ ✗
				✓ ✓ ✓ ✓

SLITHERLINK

174 Draw a single continuous loop, by connecting the dots. No line may cross the path of another.

The figure inside each set of any four surrounding dots indicates the total number of surrounding lines.

```
2  2     2        3  2  1  3
2        2     1  1  0  2
2     1        3  2  2        1
2  1     3  3     1  1  2
2  1        1  1     1  2
1        1  2  2        1
2  0     1        0        1
               3     3     2  3
1  3  1  1  2  1  2     0
2  1     3     3  2  2  2
   2     2              1  2
3           1     2  2  2
```

COMBIKU

Each horizontal row and vertical column should contain different shapes and different numbers.

Every square will contain one number and one shape and no combination may be repeated anywhere else in the puzzle.

175

◇ ○ ☆ ⬡ ▢

1   2   3   4   5

1				4
▢	⑤	2	4	
	⬡		◇	2
	☆	▢		
			1	

181

176 In the diagram below, which three-digit number should replace the question mark?

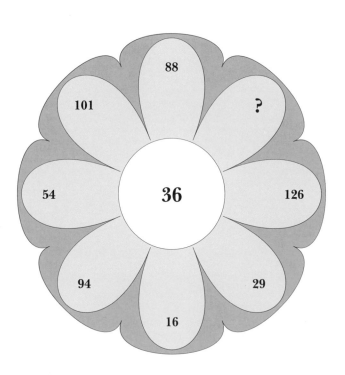

ADDING UP

In the square below, change the positions of six numbers, one per horizontal row, vertical column and long diagonal line of six smaller squares, in such a way that the numbers in each row, column and long diagonal line total exactly 150. Any number may appear more than once in a row, column or line.

177

39	25	16	34	44	11
14	25	30	23	3	33
6	48	25	47	12	7
44	29	25	28	11	38
25	25	21	26	25	33
17	17	11	17	33	33

178 Given that the letters are valued 1-26 according to their respective places in the alphabet, can you crack the mystery code to reveal the missing letter?

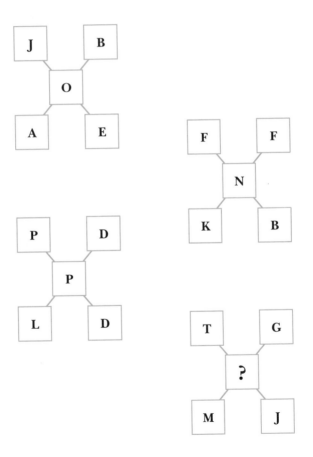

WHATEVER NEXT?

Which of the four lettered alternatives (A, B, C or D) fits most
logically into the empty square?

6	8	7
4	8	6
2	2	2

7	9	8
1	1	1
6	4	5

10	4	7
6	10	8
9	9	9

?

4	6	5
9	7	8
7	5	6

A

4	5	4
9	8	9
5	6	6

B

2	1	3
7	3	4
8	4	7

C

6	10	9
11	4	7
6	2	3

D

TILE TWISTER

180 Place the eight tiles into the puzzle grid so that all adjacent numbers on each tile match up. Tiles may be rotated through 360 degrees, but none may be flipped over.

4	3
3	2

4	3
2	2

4	1
2	4

4	3
3	3

4	1
3	2

4	3
3	4

4	2
3	4

4	2
3	3

				3	1
				3	2

PIECEWORK

Place all twelve of the pieces into the grid. Any may be rotated or flipped over, but none may touch another, not even diagonally. The numbers outside the grid refer to the number of consecutive black squares; and each block is separated from the others by at least one white square. For instance, '3 2' could refer to a row with none, one or more white squares, then three black squares, then at least one white square, then two more black squares, followed by any number of white squares.

181

				2		1	1			1
			3	3		3	2	1	3	3
		5	1	3	1	1	1	4	1	1	1
		2	2	1	1	2	1	2	2	1	3	1

4												
1 2 1												
1 2 1												
1 1 1 3												
1 2 1												
1 1 1												
2 1												
2												
2 3												
1 1 1												
3 1 1												
1 1												
1 1 2												
2 3 1												
2 1 2												

187

NUMBER FILL

182 With the starters already given, can you fit all of the remaining listed numbers into this grid? Take care, this puzzle may not be as easy as it looks!

10	70	441	801	5418 ✓	60713
31	95	517	830	6418	85429
32	128	529	831	6591	375808
33	164	541	868	7740	545901
34	198	654	890	7850	627271
38	214	668	901	8574	651321
45	281	703	1351	10921	825358
46	342	706	3356	14555	861792
49	402	731	4101	22860	891545
69	408	791	4368	55038	964892

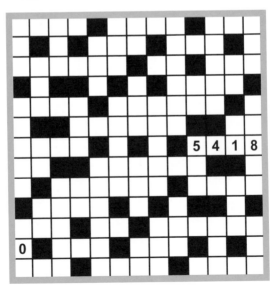

Every brick in this pyramid contains a number which is the sum of the two numbers below it, so that F=A+B, etc. Just work out the missing numbers!

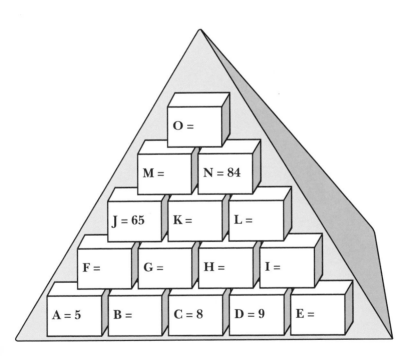

O =

M =   N = 84

J = 65   K =   L =

F =   G =   H =   I =

A = 5   B =   C = 8   D = 9   E =

TREASURE HUNT

184 The chart gives directions to a hidden treasure behind the centre black square in the grid. Move the indicated number of spaces north, south, east and west (eg 4N means move four squares north) stopping at every square once only to arrive there. At which square should you start?

N ⇧

3E	1E	2E	2W	2S
1N	3E	1E	1S	2W
1N	1E	■	2W	2S
1N	1E	1S	2W	1W
1N	3N	1W	3W	1N

W ⇦   ⇨ E

⇩
S

FUTOSHIKI

Fill the grid so that every horizontal row and vertical column contains the numbers 1-5. The 'greater than' or 'less than' signs indicate where a number is larger or smaller than that in the neighbouring square.

185

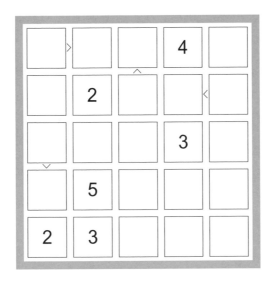

SPIDOKU

186 Each of the eight segments of the spider's web should be filled with a different number from 1 to 8, in such a way that every ring also contains a different number from 1 to 8. The segments run from the outside of the spider's web to the centre, and the rings run all the way around. Some numbers are already in place. Can you fill in the rest?

LETTER LOCATOR

Every oval shape in this diagram contains a different letter of the alphabet from A to K inclusive. Use the clues to determine their locations. Reference in the clues to 'due' means in any location along the same horizontal or vertical line.

1 The A is due east of the F, and due south of the I.

2 The E is due south of the C, and due east of the D.

3 Both the F and the D are further north than the G.

4 The I is further east than the C.

5 The J is due east of the B, which is next to and due south of the H.

6 The K is next to and due south of the G.

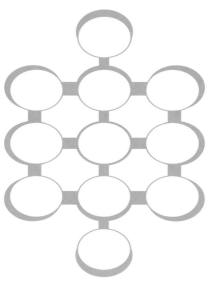

187

SUM CIRCLE

188 Fill the three empty circles with the symbols +, − and x in some order, to make a sum which totals the number in the centre. Each symbol must be used once and calculations are made in the direction of travel (clockwise).

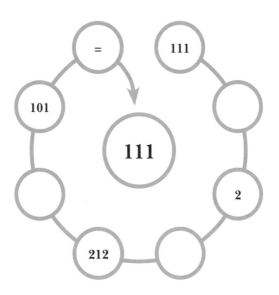

ONE TO NINE

Using the numbers below, complete these six equations (three reading across and three reading downwards). Every number is used once.

$$2 \qquad 3 \qquad 4$$
$$6 \qquad 7 \qquad 8 \qquad 9$$

	X		–		=	25
+	■	X	■	–		
5	X		–		=	28
X	■	–	■	X		
	X		+	1	=	28
=		=		=		
27		39		5		

195

WORK IT OUT

190   In the grid below, which number should replace the question mark?

7	5	11	13	21	32	10
12	14	10	22	26	42	64
2	24	21	15	33	39	63
9	4	36	?	20	44	52
15	18	6	48	35	25	55
6	30	27	8	60	42	30
10	12	45	36	10	72	49

Symbol Sums

Each symbol stands for a different number. In order to reach the correct total at the end of each row and column, what is the value of the circle, cross, pentagon, square and star?

191

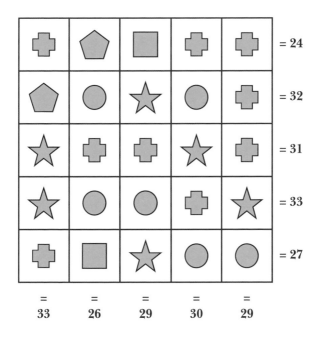

cross	pentagon	square	cross	cross	= 24
pentagon	circle	star	circle	cross	= 32
star	cross	cross	star	cross	= 31
star	circle	circle	cross	star	= 33
cross	square	star	circle	circle	= 27
= 33	= 26	= 29	= 30	= 29	

Logi-6

192 Every row and column of this grid should contain one each of the numbers 1, 2, 3, 4, 5 and 6. Each of the six shapes (marked by thicker lines) should also contain one each of the numbers 1, 2, 3, 4, 5 and 6. Can you complete the grid?

	6	1		3	
3					
6	1	3	4	2	
		2		6	

DOMINO PLACEMENT

A standard set of 28 dominoes has been laid out as shown. Can you draw in the edges of them all? The check-box is provided as an aid and the domino already placed will help.

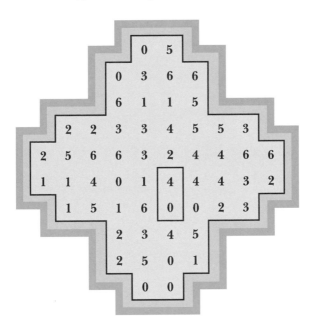

0-0	0-1	0-2	0-3	0-4	0-5	0-6	1-1	1-2	1-3	1-4	1-5	1-6	2-2
				✓									

2-3	2-4	2-5	2-6	3-3	3-4	3-5	3-6	4-4	4-5	4-6	5-5	5-6	6-6

BALANCING THE SCALES

194 Given that scales A and B balance perfectly, how many hearts are needed to balance scale C?

SHAPE UP

Every row and column in this grid originally contained one heart, one club, one diamond, one spade and two blank squares, although not necessarily in that order.

195

Every symbol with a black arrow refers to the first of the four symbols encountered when travelling in the direction of the arrow. Every symbol with a white arrow refers to the second of the four symbols encountered in the direction of the arrow.

Can you complete the original grid?

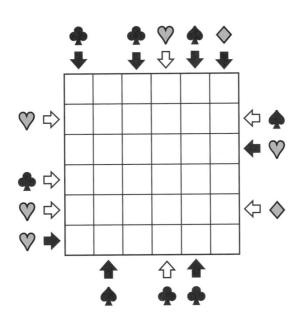

TOTAL CONCENTRATION

196

The blank squares below should be filled with whole numbers between 1 and 30 inclusive, any of which may occur more than once, or not at all.

The numbers in every horizontal row add up to the totals on the right, as do the two long diagonal lines; whilst those in every vertical column add up to the totals along the bottom.

							110
23	8	21		7		17	101
17		24	9	20		22	126
15	2		9	28	10		81
	10	6		19	29	30	121
27		3	11		20	14	103
19	14		18		25	22	125
	26	13	25	21	4	18	131
136	**109**	**98**	**100**	**112**	**109**	**124**	**129**

WHATEVER NEXT?

Draw in the missing hands on the final clock.

197

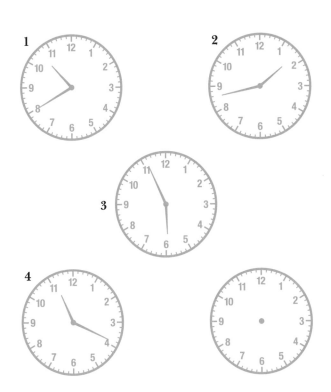

HEXAGONY

198

Can you place the hexagons into the grid, so that where any hexagon touches another along a straight line, the number in both triangles is the same? No rotation of any hexagon is allowed!

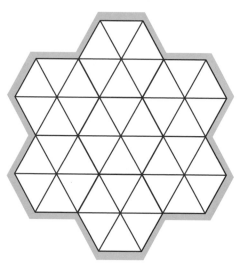

Ls in Place

Twelve L-shapes like the ones here need to be inserted in the grid and each L has one hole in it.

There are three pieces of each of the four kinds shown here and any piece may be turned or flipped over before being put in the grid. No pieces of the same kind may touch, even at a corner.

The pieces fit together so well that you cannot see any spaces between them; only the holes show.

Can you tell where the Ls are?

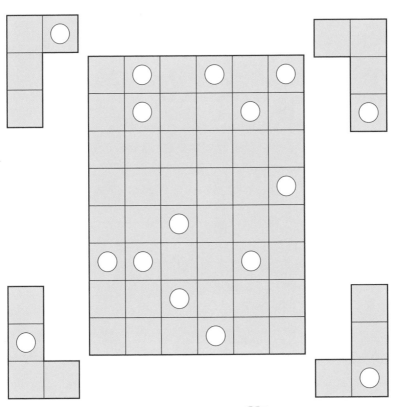

Coin Collecting

200 In this puzzle, an amateur coin collector has been out with his metal detector, searching for booty. He didn't have time to dig up all the coins he found, so he made a grid map, showing their locations, in the hope that if he loses the map, at least no-one else will be able to understand it…

Those squares containing numbers are empty, but where a number appears in a square, it indicates how many coins are located in the squares (up to a maximum of eight) surrounding the numbered one, touching it at any corner or side. There is only one coin in any individual square.

Place a circle into every square containing a coin.

	2	3			3		1		
3	4					1		2	
						1	1	2	
		2		2				3	
3	3			1	0				
			2		3		3	4	
		5					1		
	3				5				1
0			6	4			1	1	
	2				2		1	1	

SOLUTIONS

No 1

```
              4  5
           2  2  6  6
           3  5  5  5
     2  5  3  4  4  3  6  3
  1  1  3  2  4  2  6  1  5  0
  5  6  1  2  3  0  1  2  3  0
     0  4  0  0  3  4  1  6
           6  2  4  5
           0  1  1  0
              4  6
```

No 2

9 – A heart and a diamond weigh the same as a spade (scale A), so replace the two spades in scale B with two hearts and two diamonds; thus making two hearts and four diamonds balance three hearts. Cancelling out two hearts from either side of scale B (because they weigh the same) shows that four diamonds weigh the same as one heart. Now replace the heart in scale A with four diamonds, so that five diamonds weigh the same as one spade. In scale C, there is one heart (equal to four diamonds) and one spade (equal to five diamonds), so a total of nine diamonds are needed to balance scale C.

No 3

◇			♡	♠	♣
	♣		♠	♡	◇
♡		◇	♣		♠
	♠	♡	◇	♣	
♠	◇	♣			♡
♣	♡	♠		◇	

No 4

27	3	14	3	22	7	30
10	6	15	6	21	2	13
5	20	16	2	4	12	29
5	30	13	11	14	26	7
18	9	4	8	8	19	28
10	25	1	12	23	1	11
15	18	9	16	17	17	24

No 5

Time moves forward 54 minutes, then back 13 minutes, then forwards 54 minutes, then back 13 minutes, so the time on the final clock should read 4.02.

No 6

No 7

No 8

Solutions

No 9

5	2	3	6	1	4
1	4	6	2	3	5
3	5	4	1	2	6
6	1	2	5	4	3
4	6	1	3	5	2
2	3	5	4	6	1

No 10

A	A	C	B	C	B
B	C	B	A	C	A
C	A	B	B	A	C
B	B	A	C	A	C
C	C	A	A	B	B
A	B	C	C	B	A

No 11

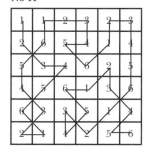

No 12

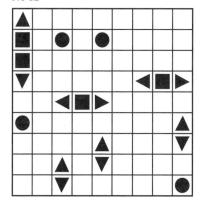

Solutions

No 13
1845

No 14

2	2	2			3	2	1	2	2
	2	2			1	0	1		
2	1		1			1		3	2
2	2		2	0	2	1	1	1	
2	1								
1			2	3			3		
2			3			0			1
		0		1	2	1	1		
3			2	1	2	1			1
2	1		1		1	1		2	
2		2		1	2	3	1	1	3
2	2	3	2	3		1			2

No 15

◇4	☆2	□3	⬡5	○1
⬡3	◇1	☆5	○2	□4
□2	○3	◇1	☆4	⬡5
☆1	□5	○4	⬡3	◇2
○5	⬡4	◇2	□1	☆3

No 16
G – The next letter in the alphabet.

210

SOLUTIONS

No 17

18	4	17	12	**37**	10
19	16	**7**	14	18	24
15	**29**	16	12	5	21
15	23	18	**20**	9	13
9	18	23	22	12	**14**
22	8	17	18	17	16

No 18

The value of the letter in the top right hand square is subtracted from the value of the top left hand square to give the value in the centre square. Likewise the bottom right is subtracted from the bottom left. The missing value is 11, so the missing letter is K.

No 19

6	1	0	4	0	4	6
2	2	0	6	5	2	5

4	5	1	4	2	5	3
4	3	3	1	2	4	3

1	6	3	3	3	0	6
0	1	6	0	2	2	0

1	1	6	4	0	5	5
5	1	6	3	4	2	5

No 20

2	3	3	4	4	3
2	3	3	1	1	1
2	3	3	1	1	1
1	2	2	1	1	3
1	2	2	1	1	3
3	4	4	3	3	1

Solutions

No 21

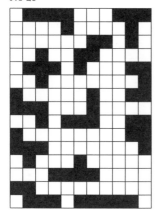

No 22

7	0	2	6		4	1	5		3	8	4	8
5		7	4		8		4	6	8	2		6
6	6	0		1	3	9	7		2	3		2
	5	5	3	9	6		6	3	8	1	7	9
4	8		2		8	9	3				8	
6	0	3	8	9	1		3	1	9	2	4	4
8		5	6	3				9	2	5		2
1	1	4	4	0	4		2	4	1	4	6	3
	1				5	7	1		7		5	6
5	6	9	9	5	6		1	8	4	9	6	
7		4	3		9	7	2	9		3	0	7
	2	7	2	7		5		3	4		0
7	6	4	7		8	9	5		7	0	5	2

No 23

A=7, B=5, C=10, D=4, E=9, F=12,
G=15, H=14, I=13, J=27, K=29, L=27,
M=56, N=56, O=112.

No 24

1E	1E	2S	1E	2S
1S	1W	1E	2S	2W
2N	2E		2N	1N
2E	2N	1W	1E	1S
1N	1W	1E	2W	2W

No 25

4	5	2	1	3
1	4	5	3	2
5	3	1	2	4
2	1	3	4	5
3	2	4	5	1

SOLUTIONS

No 26

No 27

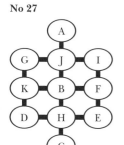

No 28

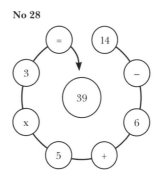

SOLUTIONS

No 29

7	+	5	÷	3	=	4
+		−		−		
8	−	1	x	2	=	14
−		x		+		
4	x	6	+	9	=	33
=		=		=		
11		24		10		

No 30

35 – The 7x7 grid contains all the numbers from 1 to 49 and the only number missing is 35.

No 31

Circle = 3, cross = 5, pentagon = 4, square = 9, star = 6

No 32

6	1	3	5	4	2
1	2	4	6	5	3
2	3	5	1	6	4
3	4	6	2	1	5
5	6	2	4	3	1
4	5	1	3	2	6

SOLUTIONS

No 33

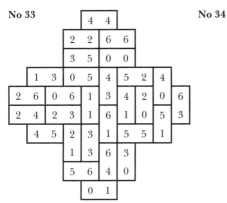

No 34

No 35

No 36

25	23	6	30	7	22	17
1	23	5	16	4	10	22
15	14	19	30	29	21	2
9	29	24	20	26	3	28
20	8	4	26	1	21	27
25	13	3	12	6	2	11
24	5	28	18	27	7	19

SOLUTIONS

No 37
D

No 38

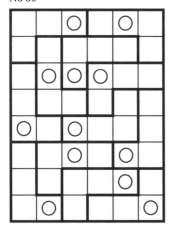

No 39

No 40

	1		1	0				●	●
	2	●				2	3	●	3
	3	●	2	1	●		●		2
	●		3	4		3	1	3	●
3	●	6	●	●	●		0	2	●
2	●	●	●	●		2	1		
		4	4	●		●	2	3	●
●	●	3					2	●	●
2	3	●	●	1	0		2	3	3
0								●	

SOLUTIONS

No 41

1	5	4	6	3	2
2	3	6	5	1	4
6	1	2	3	4	5
3	2	5	4	6	1
4	6	1	2	5	3
5	4	3	1	2	6

No 42

B	B	C	A	C	A
C	A	A	B	B	C
B	A	C	C	A	B
A	B	B	C	A	C
C	C	A	A	B	B
A	C	B	B	C	A

No 43

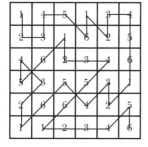

No 44

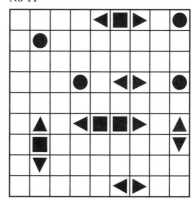

No 45

6786

No 46

No 47

No 48

39 – The number in the centre is the sum of the numbers to each side, on opposite panels.

SOLUTIONS

No 49

32	**29**	4	1	24	21
30	31	2	3	22	23
12	9	17	**20**	28	25
10	11	18	19	**26**	27
13	16	**36**	33	5	8
14	15	34	35	6	**7**

No 50

The value of the letter in the top left hand square is divided by the value in the top right hand square to give the value in the central square. Likewise the bottom left is divided by the bottom right. The missing value is 7, so the missing letter is G.

No 51

C – From the top, the rows total 17, 19 and 21.

No 52

1	4	4	3	3	1
3	1	1	2	2	3
3	1	1	2	2	3
2	4	4	4	4	2
2	4	4	4	4	2
3	3	3	4	4	3

Solutions

No 53

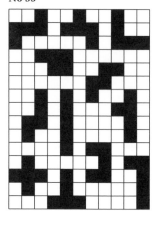

No 54

6	7	1			7	8	8		1	7	5	8	1
3		6	5	1	6	3		8	0	0		8
4	7	9		1	0	6	2	1		5	2	5
1		7		4		8	6	2			8	6
3	3	6	6		4	7		1	3	3	4	2
	0		2	9	1	1	5	3		8		0
	8	5	1		1		7		4	0	6
2		8		7	1	6	4	1	4		1
9	4	7	2	1		3	6		6	1	1	4
7	4			2	7	5		3		2		2
1	3	2		3	1	8	9	2		4	5	8
3		1	9	1		7	5	8	0	1		5
5	0	0	0	0		4	0	5		7	5	5

No 55

A=5, B=7, C=9 D=11, E=6, F=12,
G=16, H=20, I=17, J=28, K=36, L=37,
M=64, N=73, O=137.

No 56

1E	1S	1E	1S	2W
1N	1E	2E	1S	2S
1N	1E		1S	2N
2E	1N	1W	1S	1S
1N	1E	2W	2W	2N

No 57

3	5	1	2	4
5	4	3	1	2
1	3	2	4	5
2	1	4	5	3
4	2	5	3	1

No 58

No 59

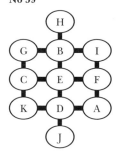

No 60

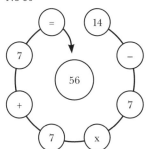

SOLUTIONS

No 61

4	x	3	–	8	=	4
x				–			+
6	+	1	x	7	=	49
÷				x			÷
2	+	9	x	5	=	55
=			=		=	
12		18		3		

No 62

68 – Reading down each column, add 5 to the first number, then 6, then 7, then subtract 6, then 5 and finally add 6..

No 63

Circle = 6, cross = 4, pentagon = 8, square = 7, star = 9

No 64

5	6	4	2	3	1
1	2	6	4	5	3
2	3	1	5	6	4
3	4	2	6	1	5
4	5	3	1	2	6
6	1	5	3	4	2

SOLUTIONS

No 65

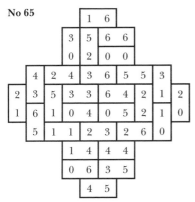

No 66

8 – A heart and a spade weigh the same as a diamond (scale A), so replace the diamond in scale B with a heart and a spade; thus making two spades and a heart balance five hearts. Cancelling out one heart from either side of scale B shows that two spades weigh the same as four hearts, so one spade weighs the same as two hearts. Now replace the spade in scale A with two hearts, so that three hearts weigh the same as one diamond. In scale C, exchange each diamond for three hearts, so that 15 hearts plus the one that is already in scale C gives a total of 16 hearts. Since one spade weighs the same as two hearts (above), a total of eight spades are needed to balance scale C.

No 67

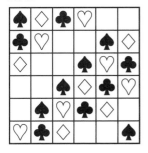

No 68

28	14	29	27	27	16	25
30	29	22	13	24	11	26
15	3	1	28	17	26	25
2	21	16	23	10	12	18
17	2	5	20	21	24	9
4	1	18	6	4	19	22
19	6	3	20	23	8	30

SOLUTIONS

No 69

There is a progression of 5 hours 6 minutes and 9 hours 6 minutes each time, so the time on the final clock should read 11.13.

No 70

No 71

No 72

SOLUTIONS

No 73

3	1	5	6	2	4
2	6	3	4	1	5
6	4	2	1	5	3
1	5	6	3	4	2
4	2	1	5	3	6
5	3	4	2	6	1

No 74

C	A	B	A	B	C
C	B	C	A	A	B
B	C	A	B	C	A
A	A	B	C	B	C
B	C	C	B	A	A
A	B	A	C	C	B

No 75

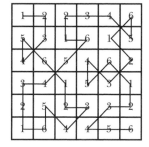

No 76

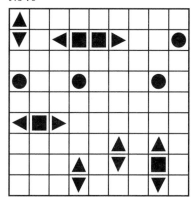

SOLUTIONS

No 77
9553

No 78

No 79

2	1	☆3	4	◇5
☆4	⬡2	5	◇3	1
3	◇4	⬡1	5	☆2
◇1	☆5	4	2	⬡3
⬡5	3	◇2	☆1	4

No 80

U – Starting at A in the centre and then moving clockwise, the alphanumeric values increase by 1, 2, 3, 4, 1, 2, 3, 4.

SOLUTIONS

No 81

20	**9**	19	26	40	8
20	20	20	19	22	**21**
23	25	20	16	**8**	30
10	35	22	**24**	14	17
17	22	**19**	24	16	24
32	11	22	13	22	22

No 82

The added values of the two top squares are subtracted from the added values of the two bottom squares to give the value in the central square. The missing value is 16 so the missing letter is P.

No 83

3	2	4	4	5	1	2
1	2	4	2	0	0	5

5	6	1	6	3	6	0
4	0	5	6	3	4	4

5	2	5	2	3	0	1
3	0	5	6	0	0	4

4	1	6	2	1	5	2
3	6	3	1	1	6	3

No 84

1	1	1	4	4	2
4	2	2	1	1	2
4	2	2	1	1	2
1	3	3	2	2	1
1	3	3	2	2	1
3	4	4	4	4	2

SOLUTIONS

No 85

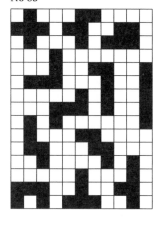

No 86

8	7	4		2	7	8		3	4	7		1
5	0	7		6	3	3	6	5		9	1	4
6	8	2	3	8		2		5	4	0	0	3
5		9		2	7	5	9	6		8	5	
3	4	0	3	0		6	0		9	8	7	1
	0		0		4	9	4	9	5			8
4	2	2	4	3	1		5	0	2	7	3	0
6			3	3	2	7	6		7		9	
7	2	5	0		6	6		1	9	7	0	1
	2	6		8	5	3	9	0		8		5
5	4	9	0	9		8		1	3	0	6	2
4	6	5		9	9	8	9	8		6	2	7
4		1	9	0		9	4	3		7	8	0

No 87

A=10, B=9, C=13, D=16, E=11, F=19,
G=22, H=29, I=27, J=41, K=51, L=56,
M=92, N=107, O=199.

No 88

3E	1E	2E	2W	2S
1N	3E	1E	1S	2W
1N	1E		2W	2S
1N	1E	1S	2W	1W
1N	3N	1W	3W	1N

No 89

1	5 > 4	2	3
3	1	2 < 4	5
4	3	5	1	2
5 > 2	1 < 3 < 4
2	4 > 3 < 5	1

No 90

No 91

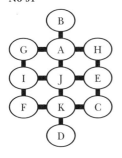

No 92

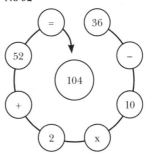

SOLUTIONS

No 93

9	+	8	x	5	=	85
–		x		x		
6	÷	2	+	4	=	7
x		–		+		
3	+	1	x	7	=	28
=		=		=		
9		15		27		

No 94

24 – Reading across, from the top left-hand corner, the first row are all multiples of 3, the second row numbers are multiples of 5, then 6, then 4, then 2, then 7, and finally of 8, all numbers being the lowest 7 of each multiplication table.

No 95

Circle = 7, cross = 3, pentagon = 5, square = 9, star = 6

No 96

2	1	3	4	5	6
4	3	5	6	1	2
5	4	6	1	2	3
6	5	1	2	3	4
1	6	2	3	4	5
3	2	4	5	6	1

SOLUTIONS

No 97

		0	3		
	0	1	0	0	
	3	6	5	6	

6	6	2	4	3	5	1	2	
2	5	6	0	4	3	3	1	1	2	2
1	4	1	6	2	6	2	1	1	5	2	2
0	5	4	5	3	3	4	4

	2	5	1	
	0	6	5	4
	0	3	

No 98

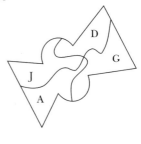

No 99

◇			♣	♠	♡
	♠	♡		◇	♣
♡			◇	♣	♠
♣	♡	♠			◇
♠	◇	♣	♡		
	♣	◇	♠	♡	

No 100

17	5	2	20	21	8	20
3	5	13	16	19	19	22
23	1	9	4	14	7	8
30	13	15	15	23	10	18
12	29	27	6	7	18	24
22	9	11	16	11	21	17
12	28	14	26	10	25	6

SOLUTIONS

No 101
F

No 102

No 103

No 104

SOLUTIONS

No 105

3	2	4	1	5	6
2	1	3	6	4	5
4	6	2	5	1	3
1	5	6	2	3	4
5	3	1	4	6	2
6	4	5	3	2	1

No 106

C	A	C	B	A	B
B	C	A	C	A	B
A	C	B	C	B	A
A	B	B	A	C	C
B	A	C	A	B	C
C	B	A	B	C	A

No 107

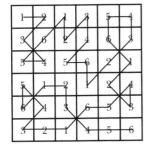

No 108

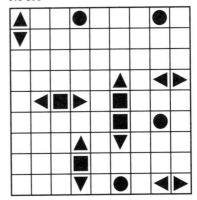

No 109

4422

No 110

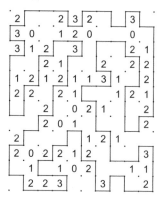

No 111

☆3	4	⑤	⟨1⟩	⟨2⟩
5	⟨1⟩	⟨4⟩	☆2	③
①	⟨3⟩	2	⟨5⟩	☆4
⟨2⟩	☆5	⟨3⟩	④	1
⟨4⟩	②	☆1	3	⟨5⟩

No 112

45 – Opposite points of the star add up to the central figure.

SOLUTIONS

No 113

16	5	17	37	54	**8**
38	22	**17**	10	27	23
24	37	22	20	**14**	20
21	37	27	**24**	5	23
9	26	30	36	13	23
29	**10**	24	10	24	40

No 114

The top array has values which drop by 6 each time, moving from the top left hand square clockwise and into the central square. The next array's values drop by 5, the next by 4 and finally by 3. The missing value is 6 so the letter is F.

No 115

B – The sum total of all nine digits is 97.

No 116

4	1	1	2	2	3
4	1	1	3	3	1
4	1	1	3	3	1
1	2	2	3	3	4
1	2	2	3	3	4
4	4	4	2	2	3

SOLUTIONS

No 117

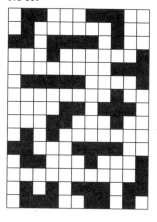

No 118

2	4	8	0	■	4	5	7	9	■	7	9	0
4	■	4	■	1	4	5	■	8	■	3	6	■
7	6	0	9	9	■	6	■	8	0	0	4	7
2	0	■	2	6	7	7	3	3	■	9	5	6
4	3	6	5	■	8	■	4	■	2	7	6	8
■	■	5	■	4	0	4	9	4	0	■	■	5
3	8	0	5	9	■	■	■	3	7	9	6	2
6	■	■	4	5	2	5	1	2	■	0	■	■
8	6	9	1	■	6	■	9	■	3	0	5	6
7	1	9	■	8	3	2	1	4	4	■	4	5
3	1	5	6	7	■	8	■	5	6	2	7	9
■	2	3	■	0	■	8	1	5	■	5	■	0
3	0	1	■	7	0	9	4	■	9	8	7	0

No 119

A=16, B=13, C=8, D=15, E=19, F=29, G=21, H=23, I=34, J=50, K=44, L=57, M=94, N=101, O=195.

No 120

1S	1W	1E	1E	1S
2E	3S	1E	2W	3S
2E	1S	■	3W	3W
3E	3N	3N	1E	2W
1N	1E	1E	2N	2N

No 121

2	5 >	4 >	1	3
3	2	5 >	4	1
5 >	4 >	1	3	2
4	1	3	2	< 5
1	3 >	2	< 5	4

SOLUTIONS

No 122

No 123

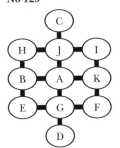

No 124

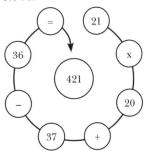

SOLUTIONS

No 125

4	x	6	+	1	=	25
x	■	x	■	x		
7	x	9	+	2	=	65
–	■	–	■	x		
8	+	3	+	5	=	16
=		=		=		
20		51		10		

No 126

12 – Reading across, in each row the highest number shown is the sum total of all the other numbers.

No 127

Circle = 1, cross = 4, pentagon = 6, square = 2, star = 3

No 128

6	2	1	3	4	5
4	6	5	1	2	3
3	5	4	6	1	2
2	4	3	5	6	1
5	1	6	2	3	4
1	3	2	4	5	6

No 129

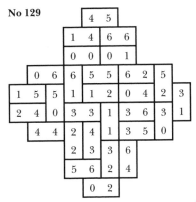

No 130

5 – Two hearts and a spade weigh the same as a diamond, so replace the diamond in scale B with two hearts and a spade, so that three spades weigh the same as two hearts plus one spade plus one heart. Now remove one spade from either side of scale B, to show that three hearts weigh the same as two spades. Replace the diamond in scale C with two hearts and a spade, so there are now two hearts plus two spades in scale C. Now replace the two spades in scale C with three hearts (which weigh the same as two spades, above). Thus there are now five hearts in scale C, so five hearts are needed to balance scale C.

No 131

No 132

14	8	2	12	26	28	27
1	13	25	16	11	9	15
17	1	26	6	3	7	29
5	30	18	24	30	10	21
29	23	25	9	5	27	7
22	4	3	28	19	24	21
11	4	6	2	8	10	20

SOLUTIONS

No 133

Clocks lose 4 hours 16 minutes, 3 hours 14 minutes, 2 hours 12 minutes, and one hour 10 minutes progressively (or, as an alternative, they gain 7 hours 44 minutes, 8 hours 46 minutes, 9 hours 48 minutes and 10 hours 50 minutes progressively), so the time on the final clock should read 8.08.

No 134

No 135

No 136

SOLUTIONS

No 137

2	1	5	6	4	3
6	5	4	2	3	1
3	6	2	5	1	4
5	3	1	4	6	2
4	2	3	1	5	6
1	4	6	3	2	5

No 138

A	C	B	A	B	C
C	B	A	C	A	B
B	A	C	B	C	A
B	A	C	B	C	A
C	B	A	C	A	B
A	C	B	A	B	C

No 139

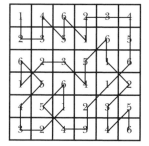

No 140

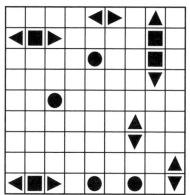

SOLUTIONS

No 141
9388

No 142

3			3	2			2	1	2
2	2			0		1		3	1	2
1	3				2		2	2	1
	1	1	2	0	2				
2	1						3	2	3
				1		2	1	1
		2	1					1
2	1		1	2			2	2
3		2	2	1		1	2	2
	1	0	2		1			3	1
2			0	1	2	2		1	3
	1	2		2	2	2	2

No 143

◇2	☆1	⬡5	○3	□4
□5	○4	◇3	○1	☆2
☆3	⬡2	□1	◇4	○5
⬡4	□3	○2	☆5	◇1
○1	◇5	☆4	□2	⬡3

No 144

O – The value of the letters in diametrically opposite triangles totals the value of the letter in the central area: thus R+F=X (18+6=24), C+U=X (3+21=24) and I+O=X (9+15=24).

SOLUTIONS

No 145

44	8	**12**	26	35	18
27	23	23	14	**28**	28
23	35	23	19	17	26
15	32	28	**27**	13	28
13	29	30	30	12	**29**
21	**16**	27	27	38	14

No 146

The value of the central square is the average of the total values in the four outer squares. The missing value is 20 so the missing letter is T.

No 147

6	0	3	6	4	6	4
1	1	5	6	3	5	6

1	5	2	3	2	5	4
1	5	6	2	2	2	1

0	6	2	3	3	2	4
3	0	1	3	1	0	5

0	0	4	4	3	0	5
4	0	2	4	6	5	1

No 148

1	3	3	3	3	4
3	2	2	1	1	4
3	2	2	1	1	4
1	1	1	4	4	1
1	1	1	4	4	1
1	3	3	2	2	3

SOLUTIONS

No 149

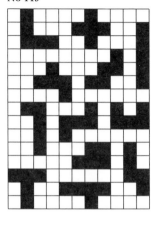

No 150

4	2	9	8	7	1		6	1	6	9	9	2
	8	7		3	0	1	0	8		7	8	
3	7	8	2	0		3		6	1	3	0	9
2		4		1		2	1	3		1		0
5	6	2		8	4	3	4		4	4	8	2
	4	5	3		9	1	1	6	5		6	9
	5		2	9	3		4	2	3		5	
1	1		3	9	2	5	2		8	3	5	
7	0	8	3		1	2	1	7		3	7	6
0		5		2	0	6		1		1		3
9	7	2	8	2		7		5	5	2	8	4
	1	3		2	4	3	2	3		4	7	
3	2	1	7	4	3		5	4	5	4	2	7

No 151

A=20, B=17, C=16, D=21, E=6, F=37, G=33, H=37, I=27, J=70, K=70, L=64, M=140, N=134, O=274.

No 152

2S	1E	2E	3W	1S
1E	1N	2W	1N	1W
2S	1E		2W	1W
1E	1E	2E	1S	1N
1N	3E	3N	2W	2W

No 153

1	2	4	3	5
2	1	3	5	4
4	3	5	1	2
3	5	2	4	1
5	4	1	2	3

SOLUTIONS

No 154

No 155

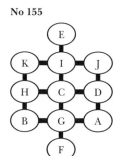

No 156

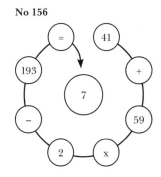

SOLUTIONS

No 157

3	x	5	+	8	=	23
x		x		x		
2	x	6	x	7	=	84
+		+		+		
1	x	4	x	9	=	36
=		=		=		
7		34		65		

No 158

20 – Reading across from the left, the first number in each row is multiplied by the second number to give the third number, this is then multiplied by the fouth number to give the fifth and this is multiplied by the sixth number to arrive at the seventh.

No 159

Circle = 5, cross = 7, pentagon = 2, square = 8, star = 9

No 160

4	2	3	5	1	6
5	3	2	6	4	1
2	6	1	3	5	4
1	5	4	2	6	3
6	4	5	1	3	2
3	1	6	4	2	5

SOLUTIONS

No 161

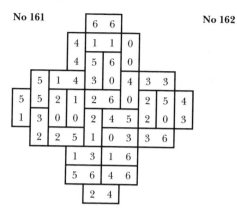

No 162

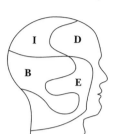

No 163

♣		◇		♠	♡
♡	◇	♠	♣		
	♡		♠	◇	♣
	♠	♣	♡		◇
◇		♡		♣	♠
♠	♣		◇	♡	

No 164

30	29	9	22	7	11	23
24	8	28	10	2	21	6
2	27	18	10	20	11	12
3	8	3	1	9	13	27
25	17	6	19	1	5	4
7	30	12	14	26	28	4
13	14	16	29	4	15	15

SOLUTIONS

No 165

E

No 166

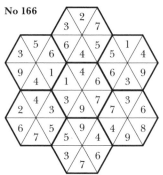

No 167

No 168

SOLUTIONS

No 169

3	2	1	5	6	4
4	5	3	6	2	1
2	1	6	3	4	5
6	4	2	1	5	3
1	6	5	4	3	2
5	3	4	2	1	6

No 170

C	C	A	B	B	A
B	B	C	A	A	C
B	A	C	C	B	A
A	C	B	A	C	B
A	B	B	C	A	C
C	A	A	B	C	B

No 171

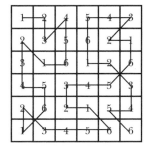

No 172

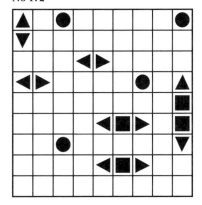

SOLUTIONS

No 173

2418

No 174

No 175

①	◇2	⬡3	5	☆4
3	⑤	☆2	⬡4	◇1
☆5	⬡1	④	◇3	2
◇4	☆3	1	②	⬡5
⬡2	4	◇5	☆1	③

No 176

166 – Deduct the smaller number from the larger number in diametrically opposite petals. The number in the centre (36) is half of the resultant sum.

No 177

39	**6**	16	34	44	11
14	25	30	23	**25**	33
11	48	25	47	12	7
44	29	25	**3**	11	38
25	25	21	26	25	**28**
17	17	**33**	17	33	33

No 178

The values of the lower squares multiplied together are subtracted from the multiplied values of the upper squares to give the value in the central square. The missing value is 10 so the missing letter is J.

No 179

A – On each row, the right hand figure is the average of the other two figures.

No 180

3	3	3	3	3	1
2	4	4	3	3	2
2	4	4	3	3	2
4	3	3	4	4	2
4	3	3	4	4	2
3	2	2	1	1	4

No 181

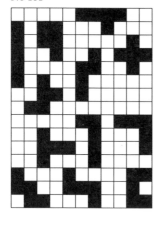

No 182

8	5	7	4			4	3	6	8		1	6	4
6		3		7	0	3		2	1	4		4
8	6	1	7	9	2		9	5		5	4	1
	5			1		1		3	3	5	6	
6	4	1	8		8	9	1	5	4	5		2
0			3	7	5	8	0	8			3	2
7	7	4	0		4		9		5	4	1	8
1	0			6	2	7	2	7	1			6
3		5	4	5	9	0	1		7	8	5	0
	6	5	9	1		6		6			2	
8	9	0		3	8		9	6	4	8	9	2
0		3	4	2		4	0	8		3		8
1	2	8		1	3	5	1		4	1	0	1

No 183

A=5, B=26, C=8, D=9, E=7, F=31,
G=34, H=17, I=16, J=65, K=51, L=33,
M=116, N=84, O=200.

No 184

3E	1E	2E	2W	2S
1N	3E	1E	1S	2W
1N	1E		2W	2S
1N	1E	1S	2W	1W
1N	3N	1W	3W	1N

No 185

3	1	2	4	5
4	2	5	1	3
5	4	1	3	2
1	5	3	2	4
2	3	4	5	1

No 186

No 187

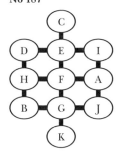

No 188

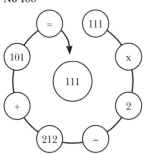

No 189

4	x	8	–	7	=	25
+	■	x	■	–		
5	x	6	–	2	=	28
x	■	–	■	x		
3	x	9	+	1	=	28
=		=		=		
27		39		5		

No 190

28 – Reading from top left to bottom right, they are all multiplication tables. The diagonal line running through the question mark is the seven times table.

No 191

Circle = 6, cross = 5, pentagon = 7, square = 2, star = 8

No 192

5	6	1	2	3	4
3	4	5	6	1	2
6	1	3	4	2	5
2	3	6	5	4	1
4	5	2	1	6	3
1	2	4	3	5	6

SOLUTIONS

No 193

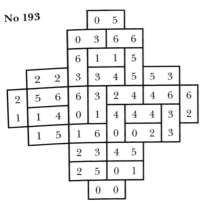

```
          0  5
       0  3  6  6
       6  1  1  5
 2  2  3  3  4  5  5  3
2 5 6 6 3 2 4 4 6 6
1 1 4 0 1 4 4 4 3 2
    1  5  1  6  0  0  2  3
       2  3  4  5
       2  5  0  1
          0  0
```

No 194

10 – Since four diamonds weigh the same as a heart and a spade (scale B) replace the four diamonds in scale A with a heart and a spade, so that two hearts plus a spade weigh the same as two spades; thus two hearts weigh the same as one spade. Now replace the spade in scale B with two hearts, so that three hearts weigh the same as four diamonds. In scale C, there are eight diamonds (weighing the same as six hearts) and two spades (weighing the same as four hearts). Thus ten hearts are needed to balance scale C.

No 195

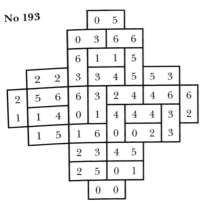

♣	♡		♠		♢
♢			♡	♠	♣
♠	♢	♣		♡	
		♠	♣	♢	♡
	♣	♡	♢		♠
♡	♠	♢		♣	

No 196

23	8	21	12	7	13	17
17	26	24	9	20	8	22
15	2	16	9	28	10	1
11	10	6	16	19	29	30
27	23	3	11	5	20	14
19	14	15	18	12	25	22
24	26	13	25	21	4	18

SOLUTIONS

No 197

There is a progression of 3 hours 3 minutes, 4 hours 13 minutes, 5 hours 23 minutes, and 6 hours 33 minutes, so the time on the final clock should read 5.52.

No 198

No 199

No 200